Jazz Arranging and Performance Practice

A Guide for Small Ensembles

by
PAUL E. RINZLER

The Scarecrow Press, Inc.
Metuchen, N.J., & London
1989

D. 47002

British Library Cataloguing-in-Publication data available

Library of Congress Cataloging-in-Publication Data

Rinzler, Paul E., 1953-
    Jazz arranging and performance practice : a guide for
small ensembles / by Paul E. Rinzler.
        p.   cm.
    Includes bibliographical references.
    ISBN 0-8108-2257-1 (alk. paper)
    1. Arrangement (Music) 2. Improvisation (Music) 3. Jazz
music--Instruction and study. I. Title.
    MT86.R66   1989
    784.4'165137--dc20   89-37127

CONTENTS

PREFACE

Jazz Arranging and Performance Practice: A Guide for Small Ensembles is a compendium of arranging techniques for the small jazz ensemble. This book not only covers the *rudiments* of arranging (such as notation, ranges, transpositions, and voicings), but deals with the real issues of arranging for a small jazz group, that is, the *structural elements* of arranging (intros, endings, accents, breaks, dynamics, style changes, time changes, form changes, rhythm section approaches, and so forth).

In the case of small groups, these elements of arranging are inseparable from performance practice. Performance practice is the set of conventions and rules that performers use to create a performance. It has traditionally centered on the problems of the authentic interpretation of early music. The conventions that enable a jazz performer to create a performance (aside from improvisation) are actually arranging techniques. Usually, arranging has been narrowly defined to include only that which can be written. But in jazz, performance practice and arranging are intertwined: significant compositional and arranging decisions are left to the performer, and not determined in advance by the composer/arranger. Jazz performers are also arrangers, whether the arranging is done two months before a performance and well rehearsed, or two minutes before the performance and merely discussed, or during the performance spontaneously. Included in this book are arranging techniques that must be notated for performers and are commonly discussed in small group arranging books, as well as techniques that are capable of being discussed immediately before (or sometimes even during) a performance and are rarely mentioned in small group arranging books.

The rules and principles outlined in this book are descriptive in that they outline what common practice is in jazz and some of the ways that common practice has been or may be stretched or changed. Because jazz inherently requires a great amount of creativity from the performer, common practice in jazz should not be seen as a set of absolute, proscriptive rules, but rather as guidelines. Almost any technique not normally a part of common practice can be made to work, much like a mistake in improvising can be made to work if the improviser is clever enough. Also, whether a principle of common practice is actually applied or not depends on the musician's orientation toward creativity and craft. If one's goal is faithfulness to a style and to the craft of music, then common practice defines what is appropriate. If one's goal is to be creative, then common practice defines the starting point for further creative developments as well as the context in which the musician's creativity is heard. In the end, it is up to the individual musician to decide (either spontaneously or in a prearranged fashion) the musical effect desired, and then to choose the appropriate technique to produce that intended result. By defining common practice principles in jazz and some of the ways they have been developed, the foundation for jazz performance practice as well as the starting point for further creative developments is outlined.

The following factors were considered when choosing tunes to illustrate various arranging techniques. A tune or a specific recording was a candidate for inclusion if it was one of the following:

- Part of the standard repertoire
- Available in some written form, such as a published arrangement
- Arranged in an especially interesting manner
- Considered to be the definitive version
- Recorded or easily available on LP
- Recorded by a prominent jazz artist
- Representative of a particular jazz style
- Of historical interest

The musical examples in this book are excerpts intended to illustrate certain arranging techniques. However, the reader is encouraged to listen to the original recordings in their entirety. Hearing the music is essential to understanding the arranging techniques discussed. Also, in order to put these arranging techniques into practice, the musician should seek out the written version of the tunes.

An index of those tunes cited in this book has been provided (see "Index of Tunes"). This index cross-references the titles of tunes cited, the artist and LP from which the reference is drawn (if any), the arranging technique discussed, and the page number where the discussion occurs in the text.

To the extent they were available and I was able to locate them, copyright notices for all musical excerpts used in this book are shown by each musical excerpt. Where works were published without copyright notice, or with incomplete copyright notice, I was unable to place a notice on those excerpts. Any failure to place any copyright notice is accidental and unintentional.

I would like to thank Gene Aitken at the University of Northern Colorado for his advice and suggestions on the draft of the manuscript for this book, as well as the University of California, Santa Cruz radio station KZSC for the generous use of their facilities. I would especially like to thank my wife, Susan, for all her help and encouragement.

I. BEGINNINGS (INTROS)

Listeners immediately begin to form a wealth of associations as soon as the first notes of a piece of music are heard. It is at this point that the listener's attention and interest must be caught and held. Often, intros give the listener an opportunity to expect and predict mood, style, and the like. At other times, the intro may surprise the listener by having no connection to the rest of the tune. An intro is usually long enough so that it does not appear arbitrary or too abrupt, but also short enough so that it does not detract from the tune itself. For the sake of variety, tunes should not begin in the same way or with the same kind of intro.

TURNAROUNDS

The most common type of all intros is a turnaround, a two-bar (or sometimes a four-bar) chord progression that is usually taken from or inserted into the last two bars of an eight-bar phrase. If the last two bars of a phrase do not already contain a turnaround progression but are merely, for instance, two bars of the tonic chord, a turnaround is typically performed anyway. As an intro, a turnaround must lead into the first chord of the head in a harmonically satisfactory manner. Some common turnarounds that lead into a tonic $C^{\triangle}7$ are given in Ex. 1. Many more variations are possible through the principles of chord substitution (see page 95).

Ex. 1
Common Turnarounds

C△7	A-7	I D-7	G7	II C△7
C△7	A7	I D7	G7	II C△7
C△7	Eb△7	I Ab△7	Db△7	II C△7

Length and Number of Repetitions

In its most typical form, the turnaround intro is played three times. Depending on its length, a turnaround may be played once, twice, or more than three times. For instance, the chord progression in the last four bars of *Bluesette* is a common turnaround, and can be played either two or three times (Ex. 2).

Ex. 2
Turnaround for *Bluesette*

$\frac{3}{4}$ D-7 I G7 I C-7 I F7 :II Bb△7

Playing it only once would tend to make the intro seem abrupt. A short turnaround played more than three times should be considered a vamp.

MATERIAL FROM THE HEAD

Using material from the head for an intro establishes a basic unity in an arrangement. While the following outlines common ways in which material from the head may be borrowed for intros, any distinctive aspect of the head may be used, whether it is a rhythmic idea, a special chord or progression, a distinctive melodic phrase, etc. This distinctive part of the head needs only to be developed slightly in order to make an effective intro.

Parts of Phrases

Chord progressions or parts of phrases taken from the head can be used as intros. Often, the intro will be the last four bars of a phrase. For instance, the last four bars of *Satin Doll* make a medium-length intro (Ex. 3). Clifford Brown's *Daahoud* uses an intro that is derived from the first phrase of the head (Ex. 4), as is Thelonious Monk's solo piano intro to *Misterioso* (Ex. 5).

Ex. 3
Intro for *Satin Doll* #1

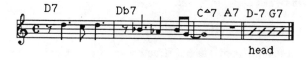

head

Ex. 4
Intro for *Daahoud*

Drum fill   pick-ups   (head)

Ex. 5
Intro for *Misterioso*

to head

Complete Phrases

Entire phrases are easily used as intros. They may be played with the accompanying melody, without the melody, or with a short solo. Often, the first phrase of a chorus is used for an intro. The C section of an ABAC tune (such as *All of Me*) is a common choice for an intro for that tune. Bobby Hutcherson uses the C section for an intro in his version of *Some Day My Prince Will Come*.

Complete Chorus

A whole chorus may even be used as an intro. Joe Sample solos for one chorus while bass and drums provide fills in the intro to his version of *On Green Dolphin Street.*

Seamless Transition to the Head

One of the most obvious but effective sources of material for intros is the texture of the head. By using a special rhythm section figure or pattern for the intro in addition to the beginning (or more) of the head, a seamless transition can be made between the intro and head. This is opposed to cleanly articulating the beginning of the head by means of a break, accents, or other methods, as is often the case. The intro to *Arcade* by John Abercrombie features a short, repeated bass line played by the piano and the bass, and continues unchanged as the head begins. The same technique is used for *Footprints*, as recorded by Miles Davis. In this case, a special bass line is played during every single chorus, heads and solos included. Because this sometimes can become monotonous, the bassist may decide to walk a bass line during the solos. A seamless transition from the intro to the head can be easily applied to a tune like *Stolen Moments*, which also has a short, repeated bass line. The bass lines for *Arcade*, *Footprints*, and *Stolen Moments* are given in Ex. 6-8. A similar seamless transition occurs on Eric Dolphy's version of *On Green Dolphin Street,* in which a dissonant horn background serves as the intro as well as the background for the first eight bars of the head (Ex. 9). Quest, with David Liebman, has recorded a version of Ornette Coleman's *Lonely Woman* that also makes such a transition, in this case in a free-time, pulseless style.

Ex. 6
Bass Line for *Arcade*

C-7

Ex. 7
Bass Line for *Footprints*

Ex. 8
Bass Line for *Stolen Moments*

Pub. by Noslen Music Co.--BMI

Ex. 9
Intro for *On Green Dolphin Street*

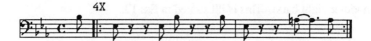

Other Parts of the Head

Any distinctive part of the head is often a good choice for an intro. For instance, the distinctive leap to the G# in the third bar of *Take the A Train* is also part of the intro normally played to this tune (Ex. 10).

Ex. 10
Intro for *Take the A Train*

The melody to *Blue Bossa* is basically a series of descending scales with a particular rhythm. This feature can be used to create an original intro, using a turnaround for the chord changes (Ex. 11).

Ex. 11
Intro for *Blue Bossa* #1

Herbie Hancock's live version of *Maiden Voyage* uses the chords from the head in a distinctive way. The tune begins with a piano solo based on the characteristic rhythm of the piece, but using the second chord in the progression, C-7/F. This is done to set up a contrast between the intro and the head; the change to the first chord of the progression signals the end of the intro (even though the head itself begins after another eight bars). This is illustrated in Ex. 12.

Ex. 12
Intro for *Maiden Voyage*

8X
‖: C-7/F :‖: A-7 :‖ head
vamp

© 1977 CBS Inc./℗ 1977 CBS Inc.

NEW MATERIAL

An intro need not always be taken from material used in the head. In contrast to material from the head, the use of newly composed material as an intro keeps the listener in doubt as to what will follow. The intro usually retains some basic similarities to the tune that will follow (such as style, feel, or tempo). The intro to *Sugar* by Stanley Turrentine (Ex. 13) is not found in the head, but is still very similar to

Ex. 13
Intro for *Sugar*

the head. However, intros also can be created that have very little relation to the head. By varying the tempo, feel, key, changes, dynamics, etc., such intros can establish varying degrees of surprise.

New Progressions

Often, a simple chord progression can serve as an intro, as in the intro to *Sugar* noted above, if it leads into the first chord of the head in a harmonically satisfactory manner (Ex. 14).

Ex. 14
Intro for *Summertime*

D-7 | Eb-7 | D-7 | Eb-7 | D-7 | Eb-7 | Bb7 | A7 ‖ D-7

Note in Ex. 14 that the seventh and eighth bars do not automatically repeat the two-chord progression. In this case, the progression moves to the dominant in order to lead to the first chord of the head (minor tonic chord).

On the other hand, an intro may be based on a chord progression that may be as complex as desired and have little relation to the head. This provides a high degree of contrast between the harmonies of the head and those of the intro.

New Melodies

In contrast to intros that are based on harmonic factors, melodies can also be the basis for intros. *Confirmation* is often played with the riff-like intro in Ex. 15 (the bass line and chords beneath the melody are optional). Almost any simple, repeated riff can be used as an intro

Ex. 15
Intro for *Confirmation*

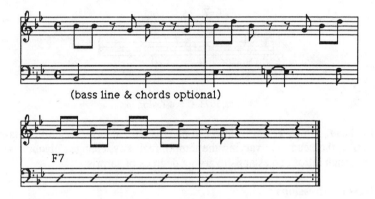

(bass line & chords optional)

© Sonet Productions Ltd., 1975

Ex. 16
Intro for *Salt Peanuts*

(Horns)

(Piano)

to head

℗ 1973 Prestige Records

for almost any mainstream or bebop tune. The intro for *Salt Peanuts*, also used for the ending, is based on a two-note melodic idea (Ex. 16).

Intros for Some Common Tunes

Airegin, All the Things You Are, Joyspring, My Favorite Things, Nica's Dream, Satin Doll, and *Seven Steps to Heaven* have intros that

are not derived from the head but are commonly played (Ex. 17-23).
'Round Midnight has two different intros associated with it: one based
on the intro used in a Miles Davis recording of the tune (Ex. 24), and
the other based on the intro used by Thelonious Monk, who composed
'Round Midnight (Ex. 25).

Ex. 17
Intro for *Airegin*

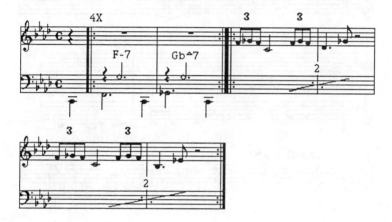

Ex. 18
Intro for *All the Things You Are*

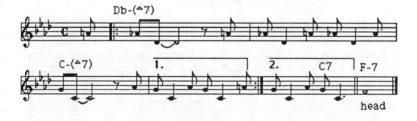

℗ 1987, Fantasy, Inc.

Ex. 19
Intro for *Joyspring*

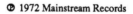

Ex. 20
Intro for *My Favorite Things*

Ex. 21
Intro for *Nica's Dream*

Ex. 22
Intro for *Satin Doll* #2

℗ 1978 Inner City Records

Ex. 23
Intro for *Seven Steps to Heaven*

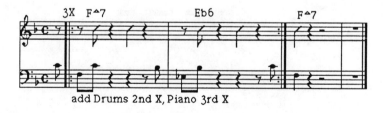

add Drums 2nd X, Piano 3rd X

© Columbia Records 1963

Ex. 24
Intro for *'Round Midnight* (Davis)

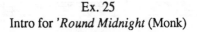

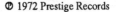

to head

© 1972 Prestige Records

Ex. 25
Intro for *'Round Midnight* (Monk)

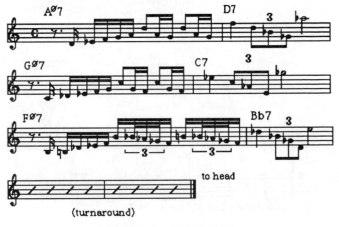

to head

(turnaround)

© 1982 CBS Inc./℗ 1982 CBS Inc.

    The following are two recorded examples that show that even the most often played standards can be made fresh through the use of new material in intros. Dexter Gordon has recorded an unusual version of *Body and Soul* that uses a chromatic line not normally associated with the tune as both an intro and as a reharmonization of the first two bars of the chorus (Ex. 26). Cannonball Adderly recorded *Autumn Leaves* with Miles Davis and created a quite extended intro not related to the head (Ex. 27). A lengthy intro can be easily fashioned in this manner, linking several relatively simple intros together to create a longer, more complex one.

Ex. 26
Intro for *Body and Soul*

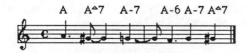

Ex. 27
Intro for *Autumn Leaves*

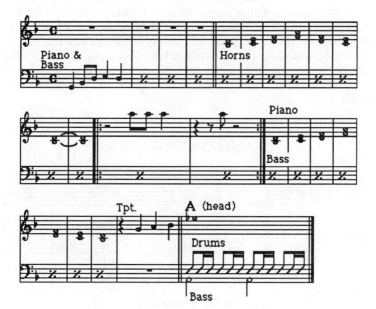

Solos

Pianists will often compose or improvise intros that are not derived from the head. Bass solos used as intros are relatively rare, but can be used effectively. A walking bass line is used as an intro in Sonny Rollins' *Blue Seven*. John Coltrane's version of *My Favorite Things* opens with a five-minute bass solo. Bobby Hutcherson's version of *Israel* begins with a bass solo for one chorus.

Drum solos are occasionally used as intros. They are often either one phrase (eight bars) long or are open, vamped solos. Several recorded examples are *Four* by Miles Davis, *St. Thomas* by Sonny Rollins, and *Wave*, as recorded by McCoy Tyner.

PICK-UP NOTES

Another option for intros is to use the first notes of the head as pick-up notes: a single instrument plays the first notes of the melody, and the rest of the group joins in at an appropriate beat. If the first notes of the melody are true pick-up notes (that is, they occur before the first main downbeat), then the group usually joins in at the first main downbeat or with a prominent note in the melody near the first main downbeat. If the first notes of the head occur after the first main downbeat, the rest of the group will usually enter on a beat that may be accented. An example of the latter is John Coltrane's *Afro-Blue*. The saxophone plays the melody unaccompanied for two bars, is joined by the bass for another two bars, and then the piano and drums enter (Ex. 28).

Ex. 28
Intro for *Afro-Blue*

℗ 1977 Pablo Records

FREE TIME

Free time refers to a suspension of the pulse (see pages 54-56 for a full discussion of the various ways this may be done). A free-time intro often ends with a fermata that leads directly into the beginning of the head. The free-time section is usually brief (four or eight measures long) and can be taken from the head or be composed of new material. If a free-time section is an intro for a ballad, it can easily introduce the mood of the ballad; if a free-time section is an intro for an up-tempo tune, it can provide a great contrast to what follows it.

The shortest example of an intro that suspends the pulse in some way would be an intro consisting of nothing but a fermata on one note or chord. Filling this note or chord might well last a long time in order to prevent the intro from seeming too short.

A good example of an entire group using nothing but fermatas and fills for an intro is *Meeting of the Spirits* by John McLaughlin and the Mahavishnu Orchestra. In this example, some fermatas are separated by short rests, and others immediately follow the previous fermata. Very long fermatas are used as an intro in Freddie Hubbard's *Red Clay* (Ex. 29).

Ex. 29
Intro for *Red Clay*

⌢   ⌢   ⌢   ⌢
D-7 I Bb7 I A7 I D-7 II

An example of using a free-time intro for a jazz standard is George Russell's version of *'Round Midnight*, which uses a free improvisation section in free time, including squeaks and noises from the winds and playing on the piano strings directly. After this section, the traditional intro to the tune is played in free time with a series of dramatic piano tremolos.

Pianists often favor free-time or rubato intros. A typical procedure is that used by Bill Evans on *Some Day My Prince Will Come* in which he plays one chorus in free time and establishes the tempo for bass and drums during a tag (Ex. 30). This tag is slightly unusual because it is performed in double-time feel compared to the head that follows it. Chick Corea's version of *Nefertiti* begins with an extremely abstract, free-time piano intro in which the bass and drums sneak in and the melody is never completely and explicitly stated.

Ex. 30

Establishing Tempo in Intro for *Some Day My Prince Will Come*

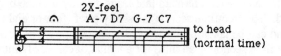

VAMPS

The main advantage of vamps as intros is that they allow more time for soloing, as a solo is normally played over the vamp. This also gives some variation to the traditional order in which solos appear in an arrangement as well as being another option for the intro. Latin tunes often include vamps.

The progression used for the vamp tends to be short (perhaps only two or four chords) and is often a turnaround. The progression can be taken from the head or be newly composed. For instance, the two-bar progression from *Salt Song* is vamped as an intro for Stanley Turrentine's recording of it (Ex. 31).

Ex. 31

Intro for *Salt Song*

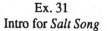

The vamp is played with a double-time feel, in contrast to the head, which is played in normal time. The following vamp, often used as an intro to *Wave*, is very simple (II-V) and comes from the last four bars of the head. A noteworthy feature of this vamp is the sudden key change when the head starts (Ex. 32).

Vamps can be extended for quite a long period of time, in which case there may be problems identifying the tune, or doubt as to whether the head has begun or not. An example of a very long vamp used as an intro is McCoy Tyner's Latin version of *Stella by Starlight*.

Ex. 32
Intro for *Wave*

PYRAMIDS

When a vamp is used as an intro, the entrance of each instrument is sometimes staggered so that one new instrument is added every two, four, or eight bars. Any such staggering of entrances is called a pyramid. The intro to *Seven Steps to Heaven* is a good example of adding instruments one at a time during an intro. The bass begins the intro, in the third bar the drums are added, and in the fifth bar the piano is added (Ex. 23). Pyramids are especially effective in rock or funk styles in which each instrument has an ostinato rhythm pattern that is repeated throughout the vamp and is crossed or syncopated with other rhythms. A good example of this is Herbie Hancock's *Chameleon*. After four bars of bass, each new instrument enters with a new rhythm every eight bars until the horns state the melody. Freddie Hubbard's *Red Clay* also uses a pyramid for its intro.

NO INTRO

The alternative to the techniques discussed above is to have no intro at all. On some tunes this can be particularly effective. For instance, because the melody of *Impressions* starts directly on the downbeat of the first bar, a very powerful opening is produced when the entire group accents that first note very strongly and then decrescendo to a more moderate dynamic. Some tunes, such as *Giant Steps* and *Donna Lee*, tend to be performed without intros (and also tend to lack complex arrangements) in order to emphasize the instrumental virtuosity of the soloist, rather than the arrangement or some aspect of it.

II. ENDINGS

TAGS

Tags are usually taken from the last phrase, are two to four bars long, are repeated several times at the end of a tune as an ending, and are often turnarounds. Either the melody that accompanies these repeated bars is also repeated or a solo fill is used. By far the most common number of times the tag is repeated is twice, for a total of three times played.

Often, upon repetition, the chords from the head that are used for the tag must be changed so that they lead back upon themselves in a harmonically satisfactory manner. When the tonic chord occurs in the last two bars of a four-bar tag, the chords in the third and fourth bar of the tag are usually changed to create a turnaround (Ex. 33).

Ex. 33
Turnaround Added for Tag

chords from head: D-7 | G7 | C$^\triangle$7 | ·/. ‖   *fine*
(with turnaround): ‖: D-7 | G7 | E-7 | A7 :‖ D-7 | G7 | C$^\triangle$7 ‖

Tags may be taken from almost any part of the head as long as they are harmonically appropriate. The tag for *Joyspring* by Clifford Brown uses only the first two of the last four bars (Ex. 34).

Some tags emphasize a melodic fragment rather than a harmonically-oriented turnaround. *Well You Needn't*, as recorded by Bobby Hutcherson, tags the last two short phrases of the melody four times (Ex. 35).

Ex. 34
Ending for *Joyspring*

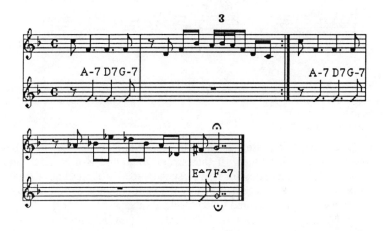

℗ 1972 Mainstream Records

Ex. 35
Ending for *Well You Needn't*

℗ 1987, Landmark Records

Blue Mitchell's version of *Nica's Dream* uses a fragment of the melody from the end of the A section as an intro, although it also can function as a tag (Ex. 36).

Ex. 36

Ending for *Nica's Dream*

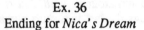

Standard Tag Ending

The turnaround used as an intro for *Bluesette* (Ex. 2) may be played two or three times. If that same turnaround is used as a tag, there is a strong tendency for it to be stated a total of three times. A tag ending played three times is probably the most common ending in jazz, and its use is almost assured unless decided otherwise.

Seven Steps to Heaven by Miles Davis is unusual in that the tag is done a total of five times at the end (Ex. 37).

Ex. 37

Ending for *Seven Steps to Heaven*

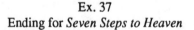

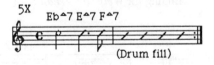

SIMILAR ENDINGS AND INTROS

A logical and common way to end a tune is to use the intro in some form. Using the same material for the intro and the ending establishes a basic sense of unity for the tune. However, there may be some slight change between the intro and the ending because their functions are different: the intro prepares one for what will follow, but an ending must provide a sense of closure for the entire tune.

Changing a Turnaround for Use as an Ending and Intro

It may be necessary to change a turnaround if it is to be used as both the intro and ending. For instance, the last eight bars of *All of Me* can be used as a tag ending as well as an intro (Ex. 38).

Ex. 38

Intro and Ending for *All of Me*

```
  intro:   F△7  | F-7 | E-7 | A7 | D-7 | G7 | C△7  | D-7 G7 || C△7
tag 8 bars:  F△7  | F-7 | E-7 | A7 | D-7 | G7 | C△7  | G-7 C7 || F△7
tag 4 bars:                        D-7 | G7 | C△7  | A7      || D-7
```

When using the C section as an eight-bar tag, the end of the C section must lead to the beginning of the C section instead of leading up to the first chord of the head as must be done when it is used as an intro. In this case, a II-V progression in F (G-7 C7) should be inserted at the end of the head instead of the II-V progression in C (D-7 G7) inserted in the same place when the C section is used as an intro. If the last four bars are tagged, then an A7 chord can be inserted in the last bar in order to lead back to D-7.

LINKING SEVERAL ENDINGS

Sometimes a quite lengthy ending can be strung together using various sources. John Coltrane put together a long ending for his *Afro Blue*. After the last head, thirty-six bars of (mostly) F minor are followed by an augmentation of a chord progression from the head. This

augmentation is repeated three times and leads to the final fermatas that
end the tune (Ex. 39).

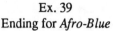

Ex. 39
Ending for *Afro-Blue*

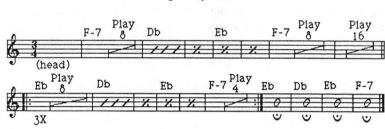

CLICHÉ ENDINGS

The tag ending played three times (mentioned earlier) is a cliché
due to its widespread use. Several other endings are also clichés
because they are instantly recognizable. Ex. 40 shows (1) a standard
ending for a slow blues, (2) a classic ending used with *Take the A Train*
(or a simple II-V turnaround tag), and (3) an ending in the style of
Count Basie.

FERMATAS

Even though it is a very common ending, a fermata on the final
chord or note is often a good choice for an ending. There is a tendency
to overuse this ending, however. After a group has put together several
sets of material, it is a good idea to check that this ending is not used
too many times.

Fermata on Last Note of Melody

Often, the ending fermata occurs on the last note of the melody.
This kind of ending is very simple, but can be applied effectively to
many tunes. In *Giant Steps*, as recorded by John Coltrane, a fermata on
the last note of the melody provides a greatly needed point of rest at the
end of a demanding piece.

Ex. 40
Cliché Endings

A fermata on the last note of the melody may be followed by other fermatas. *Autumn Leaves* by McCoy Tyner uses a fermata on the last note of the melody, which is followed by another fermata that actually ends the tune.

Fermatas with Cadenzas

Cadenzas are used often with fermatas and give a soloist one last opportunity to be featured. The cadenza usually precedes (and less often follows) an ending fermata. The former is frequently played in *Night in Tunisia* (Ex. 41).

Ex. 41
Ending for *Night in Tunisia*

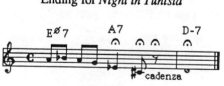

STACCATO

The main alternative to ending a tune with a fermata is to use a staccato articulation. This produces a clean, precise ending. Any melody that ends with a distinctive rhythm is a good candidate for a staccato ending. Often, a staccato ending merely uses a staccato articulation on the very last note of the melody. On a tune like *Up Jumped Spring*, it is a simple matter to end with a staccato articulation performed by the entire group on the very last note of the melody (Ex. 42).

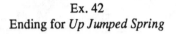

Ex. 42
Ending for *Up Jumped Spring*

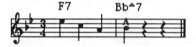

Donna Lee and *St. Thomas* are also suited for a staccato ending. While the Miles Davis recording of *Freedom Jazz Dance* uses a fade-out, it is possible to end the tune with a staccato accent on the quarter note after the last note of the melody (on beat four), the same place where the piano accents the end of each phrase on the recording (Ex. 43).

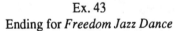

Ex. 43
Ending for *Freedom Jazz Dance*

Accents with Staccato Endings

In general, there are three ways in which accents in the melody may be used to accentuate a staccato ending (illustrated in Ex. 44 using the ending of *Straight No Chaser*):

1. No notes accented except the last one

2. An accent only on those notes that outline the last phrase

3. An accent on every note in the last phrase

Ex. 44
Accents for End of *Straight No Chaser*

In addition to merely using a staccato articulation on the last note of the melody, staccato endings may also use a staccato articulation on the last note of an accent that follows the last note of the melody. *Pent-Up House* by Sonny Rollins is an example of this type of ending (Ex. 45).

Ex. 45
Ending for *Pent-Up House*

bar: 13

© 1975, Prestige Records

VAMPS

Vamps at the end of a tune most often indefinitely repeat a turn-around or a tag. When used as an ending, the cue needed to end the vamp is also the cue that ends the tune. Because there will usually be a solo during the ending vamp, the soloist has the main responsibility for this ending cue.

Vamp and Fade

Vamps can be very effective if accompanied by a long, gradual crescendo and a solo that also builds tension gradually. Alternately, a slow and gradual decrescendo may also be used. This is called a "vamp and fade," and may be used easily with the tune *Maiden Voyage*. The recorded version of *Dolphin Dance* does not include a vamp and fade, but one may easily end this tune by vamping the last four bars of the tune. On some recordings, a fade is done electronically through the recording process, rather than the musicians actually performing a decrescendo.

Inverse Pyramid

One variation to the vamp and fade is to fade out while also dropping out instruments, a kind of inverse pyramid. One by one, each member of the group stops playing until one member is left to end the tune. This is illustrated on a version of *The Night Has a Thousand Eyes*, as recorded by McCoy Tyner.

NEW MATERIAL

Another option for endings is new material not derived from the head. Often, this material is also used as an intro, as is the case with *Autumn Leaves*, as recorded by McCoy Tyner. Sometimes the ending can be related vaguely to the head. This is the case with the ending for *Naima* by John Coltrane in which the ending continues the mood of the head, but is based on different harmonic and melodic material. *Have You Met Miss Jones*, as recorded by McCoy Tyner, is an example of a tune that uses new material for the ending and has little relation to the head.

RITARD

Often, the last several notes (sometimes as few as one or two notes) will be accompanied by a ritard, a gradual slowing of the tempo. This acts as a very brief signal for the listener that the tune is ending. Usually the instrumentalist playing the melody will conduct and lead this ritard. Another member of the group, such as the drummer, may also lead the ritard by playing strong accents that serve as the cues for how to time the decrease in tempo. One example of a ritard is the ending to *Along Came Betty*, as recorded by Phil Woods.

III. ACCENTS, BREAKS, AND DYNAMICS

ACCENTS

Accents are rhythmic figures that complement the melodic rhythm and are an important device in small group arranging. They can be categorized according to the degree their rhythms agree with the rhythms of the melody. Ex. 46 illustrates four different kinds of accents for *Blue Bossa*.

1. The first accent is played with the melody--all members of the group, including the rhythm section and any melody instruments, are playing the same rhythm.

2. In the second case, every note in the accent has an accompanying and simultaneous melody note, but the accent does not duplicate the melody exactly. This accent has been used by Richie Cole and Art Farmer in their respective versions of the tune, and is commonly used.

3. In the third case, some accent notes are not coincident with a melody note.

4. In the fourth case, no melody notes are played with the accents.

It is usually possible to change the rhythm of the melody slightly if a specific rhythm for the accent is desired.

Ex. 46
Accents for *Blue Bossa*

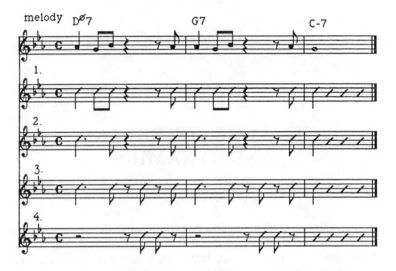

Cole version: © ℗ Muse Records
Farmer version: © 1982 CBS Inc./℗ 1982 CBS Inc.

How to Choose Melody Notes for Accents

Except for the case in which the rhythm of the melody is exactly duplicated by the rhythm of the accents, notes that are chosen for accents are usually those that receive some kind of emphasis or stress in the melody. There are several ways that this emphasis can be given to a note (Ex. 47):

1. Agogic stress is given to notes of longer duration than others.

2. Syncopated notes in jazz receive more emphasis than others.

3. Notes that begin or end phrases may be accented.

4. The highest or lowest note in a phrase may also be accented.

How Frequently to Use Accents

Ex. 48 shows accents commonly used in the head of *Satin Doll*. There are several different ways to use the accents in Ex. 48 in an

Ex. 47
Accents--Melodic Types

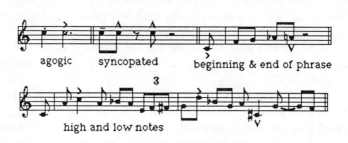

agogic   syncopated   beginning & end of phrase

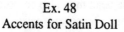

high and low notes

Ex. 48
Accents for Satin Doll

arrangement, depending on the frequency of their use. In particular, the accents in bars five and six may be used in several different ways:

1. Play both accents in bars five and six every time, i.e., during all three A sections of the AABA form.

2. Play the accent in bar six every time, but only play the accent in bar five during the last A section for variety.

3. Reverse the second option--play the accent in bar five every time, and save the accent in bar six for the last A section.

4. Play both accents one time only, either in the same A section or not.

While #4 is a little artificial and #1 a little monotonous, there is no hard and fast rule for the best placement and frequency of accents. Some regularity is generally needed in order to make deviations and irregularities meaningful (a corollary--if something is worth doing once, it is worth doing twice). Still, each case must be evaluated individually in terms of the desired amount of regularity and deviation.

These accents are further varied in Joe Sample's version of *Satin Doll*. The accents in bar four are added in the third (last) A section of the head (Ex. 48).

A good example of using many accents in the head is Pat Metheny's *Lakes*, in which the piano and bass (and sometimes the drums) play frequent accents that outline the melody, but do not otherwise comp. The frequency and the constant syncopation of these accents makes for a very attractive rhythmic effect.

Accents used in the head may also be used liberally throughout the tune, especially in solos. The accents used in Frank Morgan's version of Wayne Shorter's *Yes and No* are also played during the solos (Ex. 49).

Ex. 49
Accents for *Yes and No*

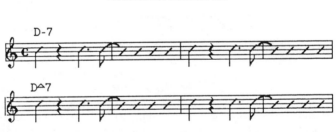

Instrumental Considerations

Every rhythm section instrument does not have to play every accent. If the comping instruments (piano, guitar, etc.) do not play an accent, its effect is not significantly changed. This frees the piano and guitar to double the melody, play counter-melodies, or fulfill some other function without harming the effectiveness of the accent. In most cases, however, all members of the rhythm section will play accents together, unless the accents are improvised and not predetermined. The strongest single instrument for playing an accent is the drums. Because there is such a wide range of techniques available (from a rim shot to a cymbal crash to the use of brushes), the drummer can single-handedly and effectively accent any rhythm. It is more difficult and less common for the bassist to produce a strong accent alone.

Wayne Shorter's *Footprints* has an unusual accent in that the piano, drums, and at times the saxophone play an accent that the bass does not play. The bass figure is offset from the accent by a sixteenth-note (Ex. 50).

Ex. 50
Accents for *Footprints*

Piano, Drums

Bass

Accents for Common Tunes

Some accents are traditionally performed in certain tunes. In the case of tunes like *The Kicker* by Joe Henderson, the accents are an integral part of the tune. Below are some commonly used accents for various tunes (Ex. 51-69).

Ex. 51
Accents for *Confirmation*

© ℗ 1977 Polydor Incorporated

Ex. 52
Accents for *Daahoud*

(pick-ups)

℗ 1972 Mainstream Records

Ex. 53
Accents for *Epistrophy*

© ℗ MCMLXXVI United Artists Music and Records Group, Inc.

Ex. 54
Accents for *Eye of the Hurricane*

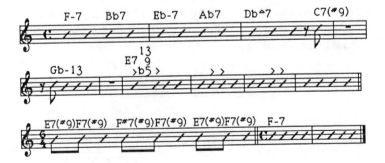

Ex. 55
Accents for *Four*

℗ 1974 Prestige Records

Ex. 56
Accents for *Freedom Jazz Dance*

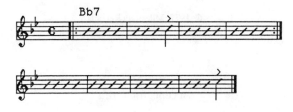

Ex. 57
Accents for *Hot House*

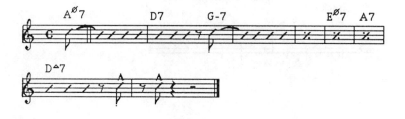

℗ Prestige Records 1973

Ex. 58
Accents for *In Walked Bud*

Ex. 59
Accents for *Jordu*

Ex. 60
Accents for *Joyspring*

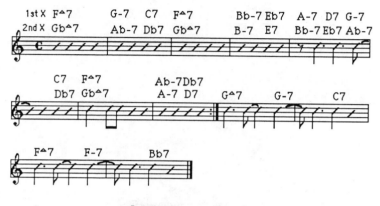

Ex. 61
Accents for *The Kicker*

Ex. 62
Accents for *Maiden Voyage*

Ex. 63
Accents for *Moment's Notice*

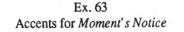

© Liberty Records, Inc.

Ex. 64
Accents for *My Favorite Things*

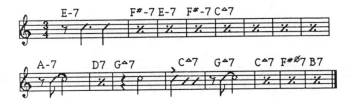

Ex. 65
Accents for *Nica's Dream*

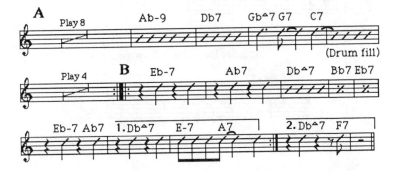

Ex. 66
Accents for *Now's the Time*

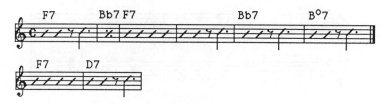

Ex. 67
Accents for *So What*

Ex. 68
Accents for *St. Thomas*

Ex. 69
Accents for *Up Jumped Spring*

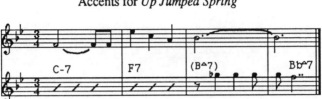

BREAKS

A break is a short period of silence from all members of the group (except an optional soloist), and provides important relief from what might otherwise be a continuous, monotonous texture. The most typical break is a one- or two-bar break in the last bar(s) of a phrase, especially the last phrase in a chorus. Often a break is preceded or followed by accents, as in Bobby Hutcherson's version of *Israel* (Ex. 70).

Ex. 70
Break for *Israel*

Ex. 71 shows a break in the fifteenth bar of *All the Things You Are*. This is a relatively simple break--it begins on a downbeat, lasts for two complete measures, occurs at the end of an eight-bar phrase, and is performed by the entire group, except for the instrument playing the melody. However, it is very effective because it emphasizes the following three things at the same time: (1) a cadence on a temporary I chord, (2) the end of the A section, and (3) the melody at that point. In their version of the same tune, the Modern Jazz Quartet uses a similar break, but in the seventh and eighth bars, the last two of the first eight-bar phrase (Ex. 71). This break is given to the drummer to fill.

Ex. 71
Breaks for *All the Things You Are*

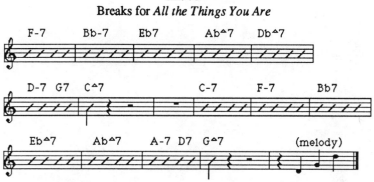

As Part of the Head

Some tunes are commonly performed with breaks that have become integral to the tune. Some examples of this are *Forest Flower* by Charles Lloyd (Ex. 72), *Salt Peanuts* (Ex. 73), *Song for My Father* by Horace Silver (Ex. 74), and *The Kicker* by Joe Henderson (Ex. 61).

Ex. 72
Breaks for *Forest Flower*

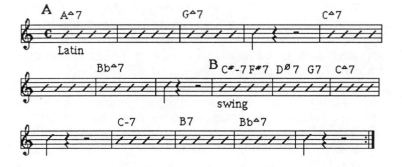

Ex. 73
Break for *Salt Peanuts*

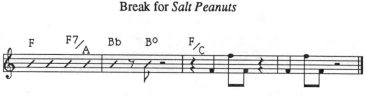

© Prestige Records 1973

Ex. 74
Break for *Song for My Father*

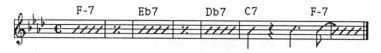

Solo Breaks

A solo break is a break that features the next soloist and occurs in the last several bars of the previous soloist's last chorus. The next soloist plays an improvised fill during the solo break as an introduction to the main body of the solo.

The solo break usually occurs after the melody is completed or the last soloist has finished. It may also begin directly with the very last note of the melody or overlap with the last soloist slightly. It often appears exactly in the same place where a turnaround might be inserted. The soloist often uses a turnaround in the solo break.

The solo break is usually one or two bars. *Night in Tunisia* is unusual in that its solo break at the end of the C section (or interlude) is four bars. However, Dizzy Gillespie has recorded a version of the tune with a two-bar break.

Solo breaks are often limited to the end of the head, which means that only the first soloist has a solo break before the main part of the solo. However, there is no reason why subsequent soloists cannot use the solo break also. It means, though, that the previous soloist must stop soloing and the rhythm section must stop playing *before* the end of the chorus to leave room for the next soloist's break.

Solo breaks may be included any number of times within one tune. The following examples illustrate some of the various ways solo breaks may be used. *Moment's Notice*, as recorded by Dexter Gordon, only uses solo breaks before each new soloist. *Four* by Miles Davis uses a solo break only at the end of the head (before the first soloist). *Surrey with the Fringe on Top* by Miles Davis uses a solo break every conceivable time, that is, before all soloists and before the last head.

Stop-time

Stop-time is a special kind of break, and is relatively rare in modern jazz, although it is very common in the New Orleans style. Stop-time often finds the rhythm section either playing on:

1. Every downbeat

2. Beats one and three

3. Beats two and four (Ex. 75)

Ex. 75
Stop-time

Any beat of a measure, regularly accented, can be used for stop-time. A stop-time pattern of longer than one bar is also possible (for instance, every other downbeat, or only the first downbeat of every four bars).

Carla Bley uses stop-time in two different versions of her *Song Sung Long*. In the live version, the stop-time section comes after several solos and fade outs. It is especially stark since no solo occurs with it. The studio version begins with stop-time and fades into the rock vamp, which is the basis for much of the tune.

DYNAMICS

As with accents and breaks, an ensemble should normally introduce dynamics into an arrangement. There are several ways of using dynamics that are often expected to be used without prior discussion. The cases of changing dynamics listed below all share the common characteristic of starting softly in order to build tension and energy by increasing the dynamic to a louder level.

1. The beginning of each solo is usually softer, and gradually builds up to a louder dynamic.

2. The beginning of any formal unit (intro, head, solo, vamp, etc.) is often softer to allow for a gradual build.

3. During the last time a turnaround is played, it is often played louder (sometimes abruptly so) to signal the end.

One significant exception to this is the vamp and fade (see pages 25-26), in which each repetition gets gradually softer, not louder.

Creative variation from these norms is desirable, but would probably need to be discussed beforehand or at least require sensitive listening from all members of the ensemble. It is probable that the dynamics in the head of Charles Mingus' version of *Ladybird* were predetermined and discussed beforehand, possibly even written out (Ex. 76). The dynamics are unusual in that they change relatively frequently (at each two-bar phrase) and abruptly (*subito* forte). Another unusual aspect of this arrangement is the harmonization a minor 2nd below the melody for most of the melody.

Ex. 76
Dynamics for *Ladybird*

bars in head:	2	2	2	2	2	2	2	2	
dynamics:	p	f	p		f	p	f		
harmonization:	m2	1	m2	1	m2		1		
rhythm section feel:	swing								stop-time

(1 = unison)

IV. STYLE CHANGES

Change in style (for instance, from swing to Latin) is a well-established arranging principle, and many tunes have been composed with style changes as an integral part of them (for instance, *Night in Tunisia, Forest Flower*, and *The Night Has a Thousand Eyes*). A style change is sometimes also called a "feel" change (see p. 49). Most tunes with style changes use two styles, although more than two may be used. Style may change frequently in a tune (for instance, several times within one chorus), or infrequently (perhaps only once in the entire tune with no return to the first style). See Appendix C for rhythm section patterns for particular jazz styles.

STYLE CHANGES WITHIN A CHORUS

For tunes like *Night in Tunisia* that have style changes built into their chorus structure (that is, two different styles are used in the head), the duration and frequency of style changes can vary widely. In contrast to heads in which one style is used, there are more arranging possibilities in a tune that already has a style change built into it. *Night in Tunisia* is usually performed with the first set of the following style changes (Ex. 77). However, a solo chorus can be performed with almost any combination of the styles from the head at any point. Many other variations are possible given that all of any one soloists' choruses need not have the same style format, nor do all soloists need to follow the same plan.

Ex. 77
Style Changes for *Night in Tunisia*

	A	**A**	**B**	**A**
option 1:	Latin	Latin	swing	Latin
option 2:	swing	swing	swing	swing
option 3:	Latin	Latin	Latin	Latin
option 4:	swing	swing	Latin	Latin

STYLE CHANGES BETWEEN CHORUSES

If a tune is normally played with only one style throughout, then in the vast majority of cases any change in style that an arranger might introduce would occur at the beginning of a chorus or some other formal structure. For instance, in *St. Thomas* by Sonny Rollins the two heads before the solos are both Latin, the first head after the swing sax solo is swung, and the next head is Latin. Dexter Gordon's version of *Moment's Notice*, a swing-style tune, uses a Latin vamp, as does Joe Henderson's version of *Night and Day*.

Sometimes the change in style can be between subtle substyles of one general style. A montuno, an ostinato pattern in Latin music, is sometimes used as the basis for variations of Latin jazz. Richie Cole uses a montuno-like piano figure as an intro in his version of *Blue Bossa* (Ex. 78), but does not continue the montuno feel into the head, which uses a standard Latin-jazz feel. Similarly, Phil Woods' version of *Nica's Dream* uses a montuno-like piano intro (Ex. 79) for the first half of the A section only.

Ex. 78
Intro for *Blue Bossa* #2

© ℗ Muse Records

Different styles may also be combined. In his *A Brazilian Love Affair*, George Duke combines a Latin-style chorus, chord changes, and percussion vamps with funk-oriented drums and bass lines.

Ex. 79
Intro for *Nica's Dream* (Woods)

STYLE CHANGES FOR AN ENTIRE TUNE

Entire tunes can be remade by a drastic change in the original style. Many times, a tune will be redone in a Latin style. This is the case with McCoy Tyner's version of *The Night Has a Thousand Eyes*, in which the entire tune is redone in a modal, Afro/Latin style. The melody is changed to fit the different harmonic context, and the entire B section melody is never stated. Tyner also has recorded a Latin version of *Stella by Starlight*. Other notable examples of tunes redone in a Latin style include:

- A Latin and double-time feel version of *Here's That Rainy Day* by Charles McPherson

- Poncho Sanchez's Latin version of *Jumpin' with Symphony Sid*

- Arthur Blythe's version of *Epistrophy* in which the A section of the head is in a Latin style

- Latin versions of *'Round Midnight, Autumn Leaves, Equinox, Jordu*, and *Take Five* by Tito Puente

- A Latin version of *Naima* by Cedar Walton that also includes a double-time feel

- Rahsaan Roland Kirk's Latin *Donna Lee*

Examples of using other styles to remake tunes are:

- Anthony Braxton's remake of *Embraceable You*, done in a dissonant, free-jazz style in which only snippets of the original melody are recognizable

- A funk/rock treatment of *Milestones* (the modal version) by Alphonse Mouzon

- The Yellowjackets' fusion-style *I Got Rhythm*

- Keith Jarrett's rock/gospel version of *God Bless the Child*

- Herbie Hancock's remake of his own *Watermelon Man*, from '60s rock to funk

- Mongo Santamaria's remake of Hancock's *Watermelon Man* into disco style

- Oscar Peterson's funky bass line for Ellington's *Caravan* (Ex. 80)

Ex. 80
Bass Line for *Caravan*

Latin, swing, and jazz/rock are the three most common styles in jazz. However, other styles can also be drawn on. For instance, the Modern Jazz Quartet has used classical music as part of their group concept for many years. Their version of *Night in Tunisia* uses a classical-flavored intro for solo piano. Charles Mingus uses a version of the opening of Rachmaninoff's *Prelude in C Sharp Minor* as an intro in his version of *All the Things You Are*, entitled *All the Things You Can C Sharp*. A rare example of a folk style incorporated into a jazz group is Pat Metheny's *Two Folk Songs: 1st*, in which fast, folk-style strumming on the guitar (in straight eighth notes) is used with standard jazz instrumentation (sax, bass, drums).

The above lists demonstrate that almost any style can be used to play any tune. However, some combinations of styles and particular tunes will be more difficult than others. For instance, it is probably more difficult to play *Salt Peanuts* as a ballad than in its original bebop style.

Even the oldest standards can benefit from being reworked in new or contemporary styles. This has never been more gratefully or skillfully accomplished than by the Blanchard/Harrison quintet in their arrangement of *When the Saints Go Marchin' In*. The basis for the arrangement is a drastic reharmonization of the changes.

FREE JAZZ

Free jazz changes many of the basic assumptions a mainstream jazz group brings to a tune. Some of the main techniques used in free jazz are:

1. Free time. This is sometimes combined with sections in time (see pages 54-56 for a discussion of the various kinds of free time).

2. Atonal or polytonal harmony. Rather than using mainstream jazz harmony, much free jazz uses no tonal center (atonality) or several tonal centers simultaneously (polytonality).

3. Collective improvisation. This occurs when most or all members of the group are soloing at the same time.

4. Melodic fragmentation. Sometimes the phrasing of melodies or solos is short and clipped, producing a fragmented, pointillistic effect.

Usually, these techniques are seen in free-jazz tunes, and more rarely in arrangements of tunes not originally in a free-jazz style. One notable recording of free-jazz arrangements is one by Heiner Stadler in which he arranges tunes by Charlie Parker and Thelonious Monk in a free-jazz style. Stadler's arrangements of the following tunes illustrate how free-jazz techniques can be applied to mainstream jazz tunes.

Straight No Chaser. This arrangement begins with a pulseless section of collective improvisation. The entire group states fragments of the head freely with free improvisation between the fragments of the head. A rhythmically loose unison is used on the last fragment of the head. The pulse begins as the horns play the head in different keys and starting on different beats.

Misterioso. Fragments of the head are used as a background to a drum/tympani duet in free time.

Ba-lue Bolivar Ba-lues-are. The melody is harmonized with dense, atonal clusters of notes. The phrases of the melody are interspersed with sections of free, collective improvisation.

Air Conditioning. The melody is used as a background for solos, but the melody is played in a different key than the head during the solos.

Au Privave. The opening melody and the walking bass are in two different keys. The soloists are instructed to ritard and accelerando in their solos. While not strictly free time (the rhythm section keeps time), these ritards and acclerandi are indicative of the freer approach to time in free jazz.

V. TIME AND TEMPO CHANGES

DEFINITIONS

Terms referring to tempo and time are often used to mean different things. The following is an attempt to define these terms in a consistent manner.

Tempo. The rate of the pulse.

Meter. Defined by the number of beats per bar and the characteristic pattern of stressed notes (jazz regularly ignores the traditional pattern of stressed notes through syncopation).

Time change. A change in meter, tempo, or feel.

Normal time. The standard time feel (4/4, or a "four-feel"), or a return to the original time feel after some change.

Double-time. A true doubling of the tempo. A piece at quarter note = 120, taken at double-time, would be played quarter note = 240, and would take half the time.

Half-time. A true halving of the tempo. A piece at quarter note = 120, taken at half-time, would be played quarter note = 60, and would take twice the time.

Feel. In general, the manner of rhythmic interpretation. Specifically, a rhythmic approach that gives the illusion of an actual tempo change (i.e., a double-time or half-time "feel"); sometimes used as synonym for style.

Double-time feel. The illusion that the tempo is twice as fast as it actually is, achieved by using the eighth note rather than the quarter note as the pulse.

Half-time feel. The illusion that the tempo is twice as slow as it actually is, achieved by using the half note rather than the quarter note as the pulse.

Ex. 81 illustrates many of the above terms. The same amount of horizontal space in every staff takes up the same amount of time so that each may be compared with the others. The bass part is notated with upward stems and the drum part is notated with downward stems. Line 1 in Ex. 81 shows normal-time, quarter note = 120. Eighth notes are swung and the bass walks quarter notes. Line 2 in Ex. 81 shows Line 1 taken at a double-time feel. The bassist now walks eighth notes, not quarter notes as usual, and sixteenth notes are swung. The illusion of what Line 2 sounds like is shown in Line 3. Lines 2 and 3, when performed, sound *exactly* alike--they are merely notated differently. Line 4 is Line 1 taken at a true double-time. Line 5 shows Line 1 taken at a half-time feel. The illusion of what Line 5 sounds like is shown in Line 6. Line 7 shows Line 1 at a true half-time feel.

The following points should be noted concerning these examples:

1. Neither double-time feel nor half-time feel varies the rate at which chords change.

2. Double-time and half-time vary the rate at which chords change.

3. In double-time and double-time feel, the pulse and the tempo seem to sound the same but are notated differently.

4. In half-time and half-time feel, the pulse and the tempo seem to sound the same but are notated differently.

Two variations of the half-time feel are the "two-feel" and the "two-beat style." A two-feel is very similar to a half-time feel--the bass plays half notes in both, but the drummer articulates the quarter note pulse in some fashion in a two-feel. In half-time feel, the half note is articulated as the pulse. Two-beat is an older style in which the bass plays half notes but the drums are mid-way between articulating a quarter note and a half note pulse--the bass drum plays on beats one and three, but the high-hat (or other cymbal) plays on beats two and four, creating a "boom-chick" sound.

Ex. 81
Time Feels

TEMPO CHANGES

Tempo may be changed either by playing an entire tune at a more or less different tempo from the norm, or by changing the tempo during the course of a tune (usually by a ritard at the end of a tune--see page 26). If a tune is played entirely in one tempo, then that tempo may be chosen from an almost infinite range of tempos, although sometimes even the slightest variation in choosing the initial tempo will make a crucial difference in how the tune feels rhythmically.

It is relatively rare for a ritard or accelerando to occur in jazz, except for a ritard on the last several notes in an ending (see page 26) or in free jazz. However, with sensitive listening and playing, a group could change tempo by using an accelerando or ritard during, for example, the eight bars prior to a new chorus or soloist, thus leading to a new tempo.

Changing Tempo for an Entire Tune

Tunes are very often played at a different tempo than normally expected. Any slow or medium-tempo tune can be played at a fast tempo. Two examples of a drastic change in tempo are Chick Corea's version of *Nefertiti* (which is much faster than the version recorded by Miles Davis) and McCoy Tyner's version of *Have You Met Miss Jones* (which is taken at a fast quarter note = 290). Less common is playing a tune at a slower tempo than normal, but this certainly can be effective. The tempo for *On Green Dolphin Street*, as recorded by Carmen McRae, is slightly slower than is normal (quarter note = 104), but still swings very effectively. An example of a very slow tempo is Bill Evans' version of *Spring Is Here*.

Extremely fast tempos are very common in bebop. *Donna Lee*, as recorded by Richie Cole and Phil Woods, is taken at a very fast quarter note = 384, as is *Giant Steps*, as recorded by Max Roach.

Changing Tempo Within a Tune

If a tempo change takes place within the course of a tune, then the new tempo is usually double-time or half-time. The tempo change almost always takes place between choruses.

Frequency of Tempo Change. As to how often to change tempo, moderation is the rule. Some tunes will change tempo only once and remain in the new tempo for the duration of the tune. Tempo changes can occur at the beginning, middle, or end of a tune. Some tunes may change tempos many times. One of the most common formats is to initiate a tempo, change it, and then return to the original tempo. Of course, many tunes will never change tempo.

One notable example of very frequent tempo changes is *Mood*

Indigo, as recorded by Charles Mingus, which uses a complex system of tempo changes as well as feel changes (Ex. 82).

Ex. 82
Tempo and Feel Changes in *Mood Indigo*

Chorus	M.M. ♩=	Feel
head	60	normal
tbn. solo	78	normal
piano solo	78	2X-feel
piano solo	78	normal
piano solo	78	2X-feel
piano solo	78	4X-feel
bass solo	78	normal
bass solo	78	2X-feel
head	60	2X-feel
head	60	2X-feel

When to Change Tempo. As with many factors in arranging, a natural place for a tempo change is at the beginning of a chorus. In an AABA tune, the B section is another logical place. In a tune with an ABAC structure (for instance, *On Green Dolphin Street* or *All of Me*) any eight-bar phrase can be used as a dividing line between tempos. Tunes that have no major phrase divisions (i.e., consisting of only one A section that is repeated over and over again, such as *Sugar*, *Footprints*, or *Stolen Moments*) will invariably change tempos only at the end of an entire chorus.

TIME/FEEL CHANGES

Time Change for Entire Group

A time change is usually played by the entire group, either for the entire tune or for some number of complete choruses or phrases. Thelonious Monk and Chick Corea have individually recorded versions of *'Round Midnight* in which a double-time feel predominates throughout the tune. In an AABA tune, each A section could use the half-time feel, reserving the four-feel for the B section. This is done in Miles Davis' version of *Surrey with the Fringe on Top*.

A very fast or very slow tempo can be accompanied by a half-time feel or a double-time feel, respectively. This provides a more relaxed rhythm section feeling at fast tempos, and an energetic one at slow tempos. George Russell's version of *You Are My Sunshine* uses a double-time feel for a tempo of quarter note = 66. Sonny Rollins' version of *On Green Dolphin Street* at first sounds like a half-time version because the rhythm section is so sparse at the beginning, only emphasizing downbeats in the first eight bars. The tune is actually done in a half-time feel at a fast tempo (quarter note = 256).

Time Change for Part of the Group

Not every rhythm section instrument needs to play in double-time or in half-time. In *'Round Midnight*, as recorded by Miles Davis, only the piano and drums play a double-time feel for the sax solo. Cannonball Adderly's version of *Autumn Leaves* uses three different time feels for the head: the melody is in normal time, the bass is playing in half-time feel (half notes on one and three) and the drums are playing in double-time feel (Ex. 27).

Ballads

Ballads can be played with a wide variety of time changes. It is particularly important for the bassist to introduce time changes in ballads. The main resources for this are the half-time feel, the two-feel, and the two-beat style, all of which use half notes on one and three as the basis for the bass lines. All these time changes will usually include the bassist filling in between the half notes. Double-time and double-time feel are often used in ballads to increase the vitality of ballads, which are often subdued.

Because the comping instruments do not explicitly state the quarter note (except in older jazz styles), there is little difference in their approach to a half-time feel, a two-feel, or a two-beat style, except that they may play more sustained notes, slower rhythms, and use a less dense texture. A two-feel does not have the push and drive that a four-feel has, and therefore the normal syncopated comping patterns are normally less appropriate in a two-feel.

Free Time

The different kinds of free time in jazz are distinguished by whether the rhythm section or the melodic instruments adhere to the basic pulse or not, and to what extent the pulse is explicitly stated. While an entire tune, such as a ballad, may be played in free time, it is also common for only a section of a tune, such as the intro, to be played in free time.

Unfortunately, there is no common usage that distinguishes between the various kinds of free time. In functional terms, though, there are three kinds.

1. Complete and absolute absence of the pulse. In this kind of free time, not only does no member of the group explicitly state the pulse, but there is no underlying pulse at all. The timing of the movement from note to note, chord to chord, or phrase to phrase is not tied to a background pulse or meter, but depends entirely upon musical or visual cues given at the discretion of one member of the group, usually the soloist or the person playing the melody. The rest of the group must be sensitive and anticipate when the soloist wants to move to the next beat, chord, or phrase, and respond appropriately. The length of time between each new chord or phrase may be neither predetermined nor regular. *Lonely Woman*, as recorded by Dave Liebman and Quest, uses no pulse in this manner. In *Kathelin Gray*, by Pat Metheny and Ornette Coleman, the two play a melody in unison, but in free time. This results in slight deviations in timing between the two.

2. Use of a nonexplicit pulse as an inaudible framework. Usually, the pulse is stated explicitly by the bassist and the drummer. However, members of the group may silently count the pulse while no one explicitly plays it. *Killer Joe* has this kind of free time for the B section of the head (the B section for solos is swung normally). The melody instruments are responsible for silently keeping the pulse accurate. With this kind of free time, no one must cue the group from one chord or phrase to another: the underlying pulse will determine that. It frequently happens that, while no one is playing a repetitive pattern that states the pulse, irregular figures are played, conceived in relation to the pulse. Therefore, the figures may include notes on any beat or subdivision of the beat. The resulting combination of rhythms, while improvised by the entire group, still conforms to the pulse but states it in an irregular, improvised manner (Ex. 83). Two very effective uses of this technique are Kenny Burrell's version of *Stolen Moments* and *April Joy* by Pat Metheny.

3. Soloist only in free time. In this case, the soloist is free to use

Ex. 83
Irregular Rhythm Section Patterns

any free or irregular rhythms, but the rhythm section states the pulse. The soloist generally either lags behind or anticipates the pulse slightly. If the rhythm section plays a sparse two-feel, it will give the soloist more freedom in which to play in free time.

Betty Carter has recorded a quite unique version of *My Favorite Things* in which she sings the melody with much embellishment and seemingly in free time; the rhythm section, however, is keeping their accompaniment coordinated with the pulse and not Carter's free time. This results in Carter lagging behind the rest of the group so much that by the end of the lyrics to the A section she is fully four bars behind the rhythm section. This is intentional, however, for she uses the next eight bars (the last ones of the A section, a tonic chord vamp) to catch up with the rhythm section. It is a quite original and effective use of free time combined with a rhythm section rigorously maintaining a pulse.

Another example of combining time feels is Pat Metheny's *80/81*. After eight bars of time, a unison melody in time is accompanied by drums in free time.

METER CHANGES

Most jazz is in 4/4, but other meters can be chosen in which to perform a tune. The original melody must be altered by adding or subtracting beats in order to fit the new meter. 5/4 is a common alternative to 4/4, and is used on Bruce Forman's version of *Summertime*. A rare case of changing a 5/4 tune into a duple-time tune is Tito Puente's version of perhaps the most famous 5/4 tune, *Take Five*. One bar of 5/4 is expanded into one 8/4 bar (or two 4/4 bars) by adding beats to the end of each small phrase (Ex. 84).

Ex. 84
Duple-time *Take Five*

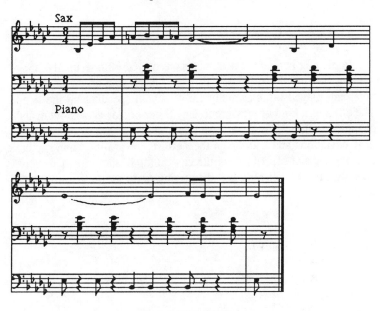

℗ 1985 Concord Picante

As opposed to playing an entire tune in a different meter than the original meter, an arrangement may include several different alternating meters. The head to *Invitation*, as recorded by Art Blakey, uses a combination of meters and feels that are easily alternated (Ex. 85). Groups sometimes are able to change styles and feels often and quickly without much apparent planning. Such a case is a live version of *Confirmation* by Steve Kuhn in which a straight-ahead piano solo gives way to a stride feel with a very heavy 4/4 feel, and other changes that include free time sections and tempo changes. Such variety is probably best improvised among sensitive players or those who have played together for a long time.

Ex. 85
Meters and Feels in *Invitation*

Head, A sections: 12/8, ♩ = 86 (straight eighths)
Head, B section: 4/4,   ♩ = 86 (slow swing)
Solos: double-time swing

PLAYING BEHIND AND AHEAD OF THE BEAT

In playing behind the beat, notes are played infinitesimally late yet without slowing down the actual tempo; in playing ahead of the beat, notes are played infinitesimally early without speeding up the tempo. The effect is a kind of pressure to play faster or slower without actually changing tempo. It is imperative that a group be aware of such slight time deviations and coordinate their efforts toward the same rhythmic feel, be it ahead of, behind, or directly on top of the beat. This skill is best acquired by listening and then trying to duplicate the effect intuitively.

VI. FORM CHANGES

STANDARD FORMS

Form in jazz is defined by the length of the chorus and by whether phrases are similar or contrasting. Similar phrases are labeled with the same capital letter and contrasting phrases are labeled with a different capital letter. Phrases are usually eight bars in length. An AABA chorus means that the first, second, and last phrases are the same, and the third one is different. The B section in an AABA chorus is called the bridge or the channel. The most common chorus forms are the:

1. Twelve-bar blues

2. Sixteen-bar AB

3. Thirty-two-bar AABA

4. Thirty-two-bar ABAC

In the thirty-two-bar ABAC chorus, the first several bars of the C section may be similar to the B section, but because the last bars are different, it is labeled C and not B. If the last phrase were exactly the same as the second, the thirty-two bars would then be two choruses of a sixteen-bar AB (AB AB vs. ABAC).

Other chorus forms are also used. Miles Davis' *Solar* is a rare example of a twelve-bar chorus form that is not a blues. Another unusual form is Hank Mobley's *Chain Reaction*, a forty-bar AABBA based on John Coltrane's *Impressions*, but with the B section repeated. Many contemporary tunes have unusual or unique chorus forms, sometimes based on an odd number of bars in a phrase.

Some tunes keep the same phrase relationships but double or halve the length of the chorus. *All of Me* is sometimes notated as a sixty-four-bar ABAC tune. Each phrase is sixteen bars long. This is analogous to the more usual thirty-two-bar chorus with eight-bar phrases.

The criteria for determining whether phrases are similar or contrasting are somewhat flexible. The twelve-bar blues is considered to have either one twelve-bar phrase or three four-bar phrases. Depending on how long phrases are heard to be, *Pent-Up House* by Sonny Rollins may be considered either a sixteen-bar AABA with four four-bar phrases, or a sixteen-bar AB with two eight-bar phrases (Ex. 86).

Ex. 86
Form in *Pent-Up House*

A
A-7 D7 | A-7 D7 | G△7 Ab7| G△7 | A-7 D7| A-7 D7| G△7 Ab7| G△7
B
D-7 Db7| D-7 Db7 | C-7 | F7 | A-7 D7| A-7 D7| G△7 Ab7| G△7

A   **A**
A-7 D7 | A-7 D7 | G△7 Ab7| G△7 | A-7 D7| A-7 D7| G△7 Ab7| G△7
A   **B**
D-7 Db7| D-7 Db7 | C-7 | F7 | A-7 D7| A-7 D7| G△7 Ab7| G△7

© 1975, Prestige Records

A sixteen-bar AABA chorus with four-bar phrases parallels a thirty-two-bar AABA chorus, but a sixteen-bar AB chorus uses the more standard eight-bar phrase.

STANDARD JAZZ ARRANGEMENT

Ex. 87 is a diagram showing how a typical jazz performance is arranged (sections enclosed in "( )" are optional).

Ex. 87
Standard Jazz Arrangement

(intro)   head   (head)   solos   head   (head)   (ending)

Perhaps the most stable factor in a jazz performance is the completeness of the chorus. In Ex. 87, every head is a complete chorus and the solos consist of some number of complete choruses. Every time a new chorus is begun, it is almost always played in its entirety. There are no fractions of choruses, and no sections are deleted. In the standard jazz arrangement, the only deviation from a performance that consists of nothing but chorus after chorus after chorus is the addition of sections such as beginnings, endings, and vamps, and these sections will not break up any one chorus, but will be inserted between choruses.

CHANGING THE CHORUS STRUCTURE

There are situations in which this usually consistent structure is changed. However, because the standard jazz arrangement is always considered to be the norm, any deviation should be arranged in advance or carefully cued.

Deleting Sections

One problem with a tune like *Killer Joe* is that the A section can become monotonous. Since the structure is AABA, when a soloist goes from the last A section of one chorus to the first two A sections of the following chorus, there are three A sections being performed in succession. Furthermore, one A section is comprised of a two-chord progression repeated four times. When three A sections are performed back to back, it produces twelve repetitions of a very static harmonic progression. One viable alternative is to change the chorus structure (only during the solos) from AABA to AAB. Even though one entire eight-bar phrase is deleted, the discrepancy between the structure of the head and the structure of the chorus is actually a minor one. The essentials of the chorus structure are preserved: statement (AA), departure/contrast (B), and return (A, the first A section of the next AAB chorus).

A more common way of deleting sections from the chorus structure involves the last head. Especially with longer chorus structures (thirty-two-bar choruses) and slower tempos (for instance, on ballads), there is a tendency for the head after the solos to be incomplete. This can occur either by:

1. Keeping solo choruses complete and deleting phrases from the head (Ex. 88)

2. Splitting a chorus between a soloist and the head (Ex. 88)

Ex. 88
Incomplete Head

1. Deleting phrases from the head: **A   A   B   A   A**
                                             solo   head

2. Splitting a chorus: **A   A   B   A**
                                               solo   head

In the first method, the chorus is not complete. This can be seen in one version of Dizzy Gillespie's *Night in Tunisia* that has only one A section as an ending head. In the ending to their version of *All the Things You Are*, the Modern Jazz Quartet only states the first four bars of the melody, continues with four bars featuring a double-time-feel walking bass line, and then ends the tune with a fermata on the next downbeat. This truncates the last head to only eight bars and a downbeat.

In the second method in Ex. 88, every chorus is complete, although the melody to the head is not complete. This can be seen in one version of *'Round Midnight* in which Thelonious Monk returns to the B section of the head in an AABA solo chorus, making the final head BA.

The second method is also demonstrated on another version of *'Round Midnight* by Monk. The last A section of the sax solo chorus is not improvised; instead, the sax states the melody, making an eight-bar final head preceded by a sax solo chorus of AAB. This also occurs on *Smoke Gets in Your Eyes*, again by Monk; the head returns at the last A section after an AAB solo section.

Extra Sections

Extra formal sections are almost always added between choruses. These sections may be vamps, interludes, or tags.

Vamps. One of the best results of beginning a solo with a vamp is the contrast achieved when the changes of the head are finally played. The changes of the head will appear fresh in contrast to the vamp that has been repeated over and over again. Merely by introducing one other formal unit (a vamp section) into a solo section, many variations become possible. *Night in Tunisia* has a vamp chord progression readily available from the first two chords of the head. Three ways a vamp may be included in the solos are shown in Ex. 89.

Ex. 89
Vamps for *Night in Tunisia*

‖: Eb7 I D-7 :‖ **A A B A**
(vamp)

A A B A ‖: Eb7 I D-7 :‖
(vamp)

A   **A**   **B**
‖: Eb7 I D-7 :‖ E$^\phi$7 A7 I D-7 ‖: Eb7 I D-7 :‖ E$^\phi$7 A7 I D-7‖ etc.
(vamp)   (vamp)

Interludes. The term "interlude" is used in two ways: (1) as a generic term for any extra section introduced by an arranger (such as vamps or tags), and (2) as a specific term for a formal section that is added onto one of the standard chorus forms by the composer of the tune, not an arranger. The second meaning will be used here in order to distinguish it from other added formal sections. An example is *Night in Tunisia*, which was composed as a thirty-two-bar AABA chorus with an interlude, sometimes labeled the "C section." Its entire chorus form is given in Ex. 90.

Ex. 90
Chorus Form for *Night in Tunisia*

	A	A	B	A	C
bars:	8	8	8	8	16

While the interlude (or C section) normally occurs every time in the head, it is usually not used in the solos. The solo section remains a standard thirty-two-bar AABA chorus without the interlude. However, the interlude may be used for solos if desired, perhaps only with a soloist's last chorus. It would then provide the next soloist with a solo break. An interlude also provides a solo break in *Serengeti* (Ex. 91).

Ex. 91
Solo Break for *Serengeti*

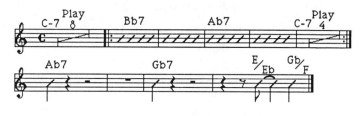

℗ 1980 Concord Jazz, Inc.

There are a great many options for using interludes. They may be used before or after solos, before or after every chorus, after the first head, or before the last head. *Un Poco Loco*, as recorded by Bobby Hutcherson, uses its interlude after the first head, as well as immediately before the head after the solos. Phil Woods uses the interlude to *Hallucinations* after each solo, but not at the end of every chorus. This provides a solo break for the next soloist. The interlude after the piano solo in Phil Woods' version of *Along Came Betty* is a riff-like melody with accents and precedes a drum solo (Ex. 92).

Ex. 92
Interlude for *Along Came Betty*

℗ & © 1980 Clean Cuts, Inc.

Miles Davis' version of '*Round Midnight* includes an interlude before the first solo (Ex. 93). *Some Day My Prince Will Come*, as recorded by Bobby Hutcherson, uses a sixteen-bar interlude with a bass dominant pedal. This interlude is added to the chorus structure before the first head, the first solo chorus, and the last head.

Ex. 93

Interlude for *'Round Midnight*

℗ 1972 Prestige Records

Other sections of a tune (such as intros and A sections) may also be used as interludes. On *Seven Steps to Heaven*, the intro occurs as an interlude before each new soloist and provides a two-bar solo break for each soloist. The intro to Oliver Nelson's *Stolen Moments* is used only once as an interlude on the original recording, appearing before the last head. *Cassidae* by John Scofield uses the A section of an AB head as an interlude between solos.

Tags. Occasionally tags are used as added material to the chorus structure apart from their use as intros or endings. Bill Evans, in two versions of *On Green Dolphin Street* recorded fourteen years apart, uses the same tag at the end of the first head and before the first solo (Ex. 94). Any chorus, even a soloists' chorus, can be tagged in such a manner, if so arranged beforehand.

Ex. 94

Tag for *On Green Dolphin Street*

C   3X

D-7 | G7 | A-7 | F#⌀7 B7 ‖: E-7 A7 | D-7 G7 :‖ C△7 | ∕. ‖

Other added sections. In keeping with his predilection for the unusual, Thelonious Monk recorded a version of his *In Walked Bud* in which, during his solo piano intro (using the eight-bar A section),

Monk inserts exactly one bar of total silence between the sixth and seventh bars.

Free jazz sections were added between solo choruses in George Russell's version of *Au Privave*.

NUMBER OF HEADS

Generally, the number of times one should repeat the head is based on the length of the head. The longer the head, or the slower the tempo, the less tendency there is to repeat it; the shorter the head or the faster the tempo, the more tendency there is to repeat it. Twelve-bar blues heads are generally repeated once (played a total of two times at the beginning of the tune, and played once or twice at the end of the tune). Sixteen-bar heads are sometimes played once, sometimes twice. *Giant Steps* is an example of a sixteen-bar head played at a very fast tempo and repeated once. Thirty-two-bar heads are rarely repeated. Sometimes a head is played twice at the beginning of a tune, but only once at the end to avoid too much repetition of it.

Moment's Notice is a special composition in that it is nominally a thirty-two-bar head, but uses a very slight variation of the head as an intro. The intro is exactly like the head except that the melody notes are sustained in the intro and the rhythm section does not play accents that occur in the head. This general procedure could be applied when arranging any standard tune. The arranger would make a variation of the head in some similar regard, and this would be used as an intro to the tune.

A rare case of a head repeated twice (played a total of three times) is *Nardis*, as recorded by Richie Beirach. The three heads are separated by vamping the bass line used as an intro. Because the solos do not use the changes of the head and because the heads are separated by a vamp, three heads do not seem excessive.

Another unusual case is the group Out of the Blue's version of *Hot House* in which there is, in effect, no head at all. The arrangement begins with solos, and eventually includes the melody only near the end.

SOLOS

Split Choruses

A minor formal change is splitting choruses among soloists. Normally, each soloist will play one or several complete choruses. If a tune must be kept short, if there are more than a couple of soloists, or in the case of a slow ballad, every soloist need not solo over a complete chorus. Each soloist may solo over only half a chorus, especially in a long AABA tune. Soloing over half a chorus is common for vocalists, especially on slow ballads. Depending on the specific time requirements, two A sections of a slow ballad may very well be sufficient for a solo. The vocalist therefore returns to sing only the last BA of an AABA tune.

All the Things You Are, as recorded by Thelonious Monk, has unusually brief solo sections (one eight-bar phrase) for each soloist. An extreme example of splitting choruses is Miles Davis' *Sorcerer*, in which trumpet and sax trade eights instead of taking normal solos.

Solo Order

Changing the order of solos is frequently overlooked in arranging. Wind instruments usually solo before the rhythm section. Within the rhythm section, piano and guitar will usually solo before the bass, which will usually solo before the drums. The accompaniment for horn solos produces, generally, the densest and loudest texture; for piano or guitar solos this accompaniment is sometimes softer and less dense, and for bass and drum solos it is generally the most sparse. In this sequence (horn solos, piano/guitar solos, bass/drum solos) the texture generally becomes thinner and thinner (until the head returns). When a bass or drum solo is the first solo, this sequence changes, thinning out the texture immediately. Examples of tunes that have been recorded with a bass solo for the first solo include *Nardis*, *Dolphin Dance*, and *Inner Urge*. Even when horn solos are first, changing the order of the horn solos so that the same horn does not always take the very first solo can be done for variety's sake.

More Than One Solo

Occasionally the leader of a group or the leader of a recording session will take more than one solo; that is, not merely solo for more than one chorus, but (usually) take the first solo, and then solo again after the other members have all soloed. This can be seen on several recordings, including *Bag's Groove*, as recorded by Miles Davis, and *Blue Seven* by Sonny Rollins. In *Cool Blues* by Charlie Parker, Parker and the pianist each take an extra chorus before the last head.

Different Changes for Solos

On occasion, different changes are used for the solos than were used in the head. Either the tune was originally composed with different changes for the solos, or different changes are put in by an arranger. Examples of the former are *Un Poco Loco* by Bud Powell, which uses a progression based on I - bII for the solos; *Stolen Moments* by Oliver Nelson, in which a minor blues (Ex. 95) is used for solos instead of the sixteen-bar head (it is not uncommon for a blues to be used for the solos and not the head); *Leaving* by Richie Beirach, in which a single scale is used for solos in an open vamp; and *New Breed* by Dave Liebman, which changes the chorus form just slightly for its solos (the B section is reduced to eight bars in the solos from its length of sixteen bars in the head).

Ex. 95
Solo Changes for Minor Blues

C-7 I '/. I '/. I '/. I F-7 I '/. I C-7 I '/. I Ab7 I G7 I C-7 I '/. I

Examples of an arranger introducing new solo changes are *Stella by Starlight*, as recorded by McCoy Tyner (which never uses the changes to the head for solos, but instead uses a vamp) and *Nardis*, as recorded by Richie Beirach (which features solos in a free, collective-improvisation style with no apparent chord changes). As is common in free jazz, Beirach's trio does have some material they use as a point of reference: in this case, the bass line from the intro. In a rare case of two different versions of the same tune in which the composer is also on both recordings, one version of *Pools* by Don Grolnick uses a turnaround for some solos and uses a section that is absent from the other version of the tune recorded by *Steps*.

It is usually possible to use the changes of the head for solos even if the tune was originally composed and recorded with a different set of changes for the solos (for instance, *Stolen Moments*).

No Solos

Rarely, tunes are composed so that specific solo sections are not included--instead, the melody is merely repeated again and again. A famous early example of this is from Miles Davis' mid-1960s group on Wayne Shorter's *Nefertiti*. The tune features Tony Williams on drums, continuously soloing while the horns continue to repeat the melody again and again. (Of course, *Nefertiti* can be performed with solos like other tunes.) This type of tune can be used as a signature tune, as is *Odwalla*, the signature tune of the Art Ensemble of Chicago. *Odwalla* is a sixteen-bar theme repeated continually, sometimes simultaneously with an improvised solo (as a "background" to the theme). The counterpoint between the theme and the solo is made possible in this case because the theme is not very active, and because the group's style allows for a generally greater degree of complexity and dissonance than is usual in mainstream jazz groups.

When playing a tune without solos, the group must be more attentive to building both small and large climaxes (mainly through a denser accompaniment and dynamics) to compensate for the lack of solos and the repetitive melody.

Simultaneous Solos

Playing two simultaneous solos presents the soloists with the problem of staying out of each other's way. The main principle for solving this problem is borrowed from counterpoint and states that for two equal melodies, one should be more active when the other is less active, and vice versa. An example of two simultaneous solos occurs on James Newton's version of *Cotton Tail*. After the sax solo, the piano and flute use one chorus to trade fours (itself an unusual technique for solo sections). In the next chorus, both instruments solo at the same time.

CHANGING THE MELODY

In nearly all jazz performances, the original melody is varied slightly through a number of embellishments. However, the embellishing procedure may go beyond small changes in phrasing, timing, using turns, and so on, and actually change the melody in significant ways. Sonny Rollins gives such a treatment to the melody of *On Green Dolphin Street*, embellishing it so much that only fragments of the melody are recognizable. Sonny Stitt has recorded a version of *Cherokee* in which only eight bars of the head are played, after which Stitt solos. Pepper Adams leaves the first head of his version of *Pent-Up House* essentially the same as the original Sonny Rollins arrangement--a melody and rhythm section accents (see page 75). However, in the second head, while the bass and piano repeat the accents they played in the first head, the drums shift over to a loose ride pattern on the high-hat, and Adams very loosely interprets and embellishes the melody. This combination gives a different and unusual feel to the second head, and is an effective contrast.

Also unusual is Bruce Forman's treatment of *Giant Steps*. The rhythm of the first two four-bar melodic phrases is changed and compressed into one measure. This leaves the remaining three measures of the two four-bar phrases to be filled by the drummer (Ex. 96). The second half of the head is performed in a regular way, using standard patterns and not changing the melody of the original.

Ex. 96
Altered Melody for *Giant Steps* (Forman)

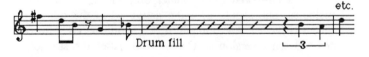

℗ 1984 Concord Jazz, Inc.

Forman's remake of *Giant Steps* can be compared to Max Roach's. In the first eight bars, Roach changes the rhythm of the melody to half-notes on beats one and three. The last eight bars of the head consists only of accents on every other downbeat in a very limited outline of the melody (Ex. 97).

Ex. 97
Altered Melody for *Giant Steps* (Roach)

bar 9

A rare kind of remake of a melody is Miles Davis' version of Eddie Harris' *Freedom Jazz Dance*. Harris' original version has very little rest between phrases, whereas Davis' version has several bars rest between phrases. In Ex. 98, the beginning of phrases in each version are aligned vertically, but more bars of rest occur in the Davis version.

Ex. 98
Different Heads for *Freedom Jazz Dance*

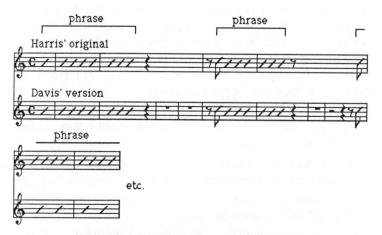

On Steve Kuhn's version of *Confirmation*, Sheila Jordan trades phrases from the head with bass fills inserted between Jordan's phrases and added to the chorus form (Ex. 99). This is different from trading fours in that the bass fills are not done *over* the chorus structure, but are added to it.

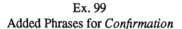

Ex. 99
Added Phrases for *Confirmation*

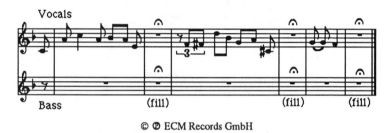

© ℗ ECM Records GmbH

FOURS

"Trading fours" is the term used to describe the situation in which each successive set of four bars is used for a short solo by a different member of the group. This is a very popular alternative to a drum solo in which all the other members of the group stop playing and let the drummer truly "solo." With fours, the melodic and harmonic basis of the tune is made apparent, yet the drummer is still spotlighted. This may continue for several or many choruses.

There are two different forms fours can take:

1. Every member takes one four-bar solo, usually in the order of the full-length solos

2. The drummer solos over every other four bars; the rest of the group solos in between the drummer's four bars, in order.

Fours have other variants. Two of the most common are "twos" and "eights," in which two-bar phrases or eight-bar phrases are traded instead of four-bar phrases. Twos most often occur in slower-tempo tunes, and eights in faster tunes. An example of twos occurs in *Pent-Up House* by Sonny Rollins; an example of eights occurs in both *Hallucinations*, as recorded by Phil Woods, and *Moment's Notice*, as recorded by Dexter Gordon. A rare example of trading sixes occurs on Phil Woods' version of Miles Davis' *Solar*, a twelve-bar chorus form.

Daahoud by Clifford Brown uses another interesting variation-- presumably written-out two-bar horn backgrounds (derived from the head) are alternated with two-bar drum fills, as if the drums and backgrounds are engaged in twos.

VII. RHYTHM SECTION PROCEDURE

The standard procedure for the rhythm section is for the bass and drums to play standard patterns appropriate to the style of the tune (see Appendix C), while comping instruments provide a chordal accompaniment. Many variations may be substituted for the standard patterns in Appendix C. Half-time and double-time feels, previously discussed, are also variations of standard patterns. Deviations from these standard patterns are regularly done during bass solos; the drums typically play a very sparse pattern that minimally outlines the time, sometimes only a high-hat on beats two and four. Comping instruments usually play very sparsely as well. Drum solos are typically *actual* solos, that is, only drums are playing.

Standard patterns are also embellished and developed throughout a tune. One important variation of standard patterns is the articulation of formal units. The entire rhythm section, but the drummer in particular, is responsible for articulating the form of the tune by emphasizing or highlighting in some way the end of one formal section (such as an eight-bar phrase, or an entire chorus) and the beginning of the next. Drums will typically do this by some kind of fill or accent. The bass can do this by playing at a different dynamic, playing fewer roots (thus increasing the harmonic tension in the bass line), changing direction of a long ascending or descending line, or by any technique of building and releasing musical tension. Comping instruments may play faster and more syncopated rhythms, use different voicings, and so forth.

In addition to varying and embellishing the standard patterns, there are many different ways in which any rhythm section pattern may be used in a tune as a whole. These methods, outlined below, prevent the standard patterns from being used monotonously throughout an entire tune.

DIFFERENT PROCEDURE IN HEAD

It is a very common arranging technique to alter the rhythm section's approach in the head. The move from not playing standard patterns to playing them provides a great opportunity for the rhythm section to really dig in and swing hard once the patterns are begun, contrasting with what came before.

Melody with Accents

Often, the head is nothing more than a melody with rhythm section accents, as in *Blue Train* by John Coltrane (Ex. 100), *Pent-Up House* by Sonny Rollins (Ex. 101), and *So What* by Miles Davis (Ex. 67).

Ex. 100
Accents in Head for *Blue Train*

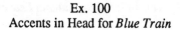

Ex. 101
Accents in Head for *Pent-Up House*

(The accents in *So What* were also used by Wes Montgomery in his version of *Impressions*.) In each case, the piano does not improvise comping, the bass does not walk, nor do the drums play a standard time-pattern. The rhythm section only plays relatively simple accents, either between melodic phrases or in agreement with the melody (see pages 27-28 for degrees of agreement between accents and a melody). It is only when the solos begin that the regular comping, walking, and time-patterns are used. The contrast thus produced is very striking. The standard patterns can barely help but sound fresh when highlighted in this manner. Even if the original version of the head is normally played straight-ahead, this technique is possible.

The change to a standard pattern can also occur during the head. An up-tempo version of *Autumn Leaves* is well-suited for this kind of arrangement (Ex. 102). In this case, the B section uses the standard swing patterns.

Ex. 102
Accents in Head for *Autumn Leaves*

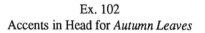

Unison Melody

It is possible for all instruments to play the melody for the head. In *Scrapple from the Apple*, as recorded by Jim Hall, all three members of the trio (guitar, bass, and drums) play the melody (the drums merely play the rhythm of the melody). In the unison section of *Spain* by Chick Corea, the hand-clap is the only instrument not playing the melody, and provides a pulse on beats one and three that frames the striking, syncopated melody. The A section of the head to *Oleo* is usually played in unison by most instruments, including bass. Drums normally play the rhythms in unison, or keep time. The B section of the tune uses a standard rhythm section format.

Because bebop and funk melodies are often very syncopated, a unison melody can be very effective, highlighting the syncopation.

Fermata

For ballads, one option that can make for a very rhapsodic and dramatic opening head is to break up the melody into its constituent phrases and end each phrase with a fermata, a short fill, or a cadenza. The pulse is normally suspended to allow the necessary rhythmic freedom. While the soloist freely interprets the melody, the rhythm section fills or perhaps accents the notes that are held under the fermata. Arthur Blythe uses this approach in his arrangement of *Naima* (Ex. 103).

Ex. 103

Fermatas for *Naima*

‖: Bb-7 | Eb7 | B7 | A7 | Ab△7 :‖

© 1979 CBS INC./℗ 1979 CBS Inc.

When Freddie Hubbard reaches the end of a phrase in his version of *Here's That Rainy Day* (a trumpet/guitar duo), he sustains a pitch while the guitarist fills beneath Hubbard's fermata in counterpoint with the trumpet.

Tunes other than ballads can also use this technique effectively. In the first head of *500 Miles High*, Chick Corea uses fermatas at the end of short phrases in the melody as well as free time within each short phrase.

No Pulse

The rhythm section, when playing a standard pattern, usually explicitly states the pulse--the bass and the drums play constant quarter notes, and the drummer's high-hat snaps shut on beats two and four. An alternate treatment for a head is to suspend this explicit statement of the pulse but still play in time. Rhythms and phrasing are improvised, irregular, and do not make the pulse explicit (see page 81). Jack DeJohnette uses this approach on his *Silver Hollow*. This can be compared to Bobby Hutcherson's version of the same tune, in which the pulse is a little more explicitly stated.

The Modern Jazz Quartet has recorded a version of Ornette Coleman's *Lonely Woman* in which the head is played completely without a pulse, even as a background framework. The bass sustains long notes, piano and vibes use tremolo on the chords, and the piano right hand freely interprets the melody with many fermatas. The head for *Dolphin Dance*, as recorded by Grover Washington, also uses frequent fermatas and no pulse. (The solos are done in time.) In Pat Metheny's *Watercolors* the head is first played rubato (a piano/guitar duo) and then in time, with a complete rhythm section.

The B Section

The B section of the head is a natural place to alter the rhythm section's approach because it contrasts with the A section. Some AABA tunes have no melody for the B section (such as *Scrapple from the Apple*). In such tunes the full rhythm section usually accompanies a soloist during the B section. Occasionally, drum solos or bass solos for B sections are used instead. One version of *Scrapple from the Apple* with Phil Woods features a walking bass line for the B section. Even though *Confirmation* has a written-out melody for its B section, Clifford Brown's version uses a drum solo on the B section during the last head.

DROPPING INSTRUMENTS OUT

Another important way to change the rhythm section approach is not to include every instrument all the time. Ideally, rhythm section members should drop out occasionally in order to vary the texture and sound of the ensemble.

During Solos

One very common way of dropping out instruments is to use no comping instruments during a solo. This can be seen in *Hallucinations* and *Along Came Betty*, as recorded by Phil Woods (piano does not play for much of the sax solo in both tunes), and *Pent-Up House* by Sonny Rollins (piano does not play for much of the trumpet and sax solos). While this texture is a very attractive one, it puts a little more pressure on the soloist and the bassist to clearly define the changes. A more extreme version of this is the recording of *Donna Lee* by Richie Cole and Phil Woods in which Cole and Woods both take solos at the same time and with no accompaniment. The fast tempo and the lack of rhythm section support make their performance remarkable.

Instruments typically play very sparsely during bass and drum solos, so it is not so drastic to have instruments lay out entirely during bass and drum solos. Also, within one solo, an instrument can begin by not accompanying the solo at all, and then introduce an accompaniment somewhere in the middle of the solo (or the reverse; comp initially, then drop out). Bill Evans' version of *Autumn Leaves* uses only bass at the beginning of the bass solo (piano and drums lay out), then the piano is added in for a piano and bass duo, and finally the drums are added.

During the Head

Instruments can also lay out during the head in many different combinations. In *Oleo*, as recorded by Miles Davis, the piano plays only in the B sections of the head and the B sections of the solos, and the drums do not play during the head at all (except for the B section of the last head, an uncharacteristic inconsistency). *Alone Together*, as recorded by Louie Bellson, uses a similarly sparse texture--on the A sections (the tune is an AABA form) the sax plays the melody and the bass walks a bass line; on the B section the rest of the group joins in (piano, trumpet, and drums). In Oscar Peterson's recording of *Straight No Chaser* the melody is played by bass and harmonica while the rest of the group does not play at all. On *Will* by Weather Report, the bass and the sax state the melody. On *Manolete, Barbary Coast, Palladium,* and *Non-Stop Home* (all by Weather Report) the sax and keyboard play the melody in unison (often, the keyboard is slightly offset rhythmically from the saxophone). The drums and bass typically are very active beneath these unison melodies. Carmen McRae's version of *Satin Doll* uses only bass and vocals for the head, creating two independent and nearly equal melodies in counterpoint.

DEVIATIONS FROM STANDARD PATTERNS

One important function for bass and drums is to explicitly state the pulse through the standard patterns or their variations. When the bass and/or the drums are not playing these patterns, how and whether the pulse is explicated is changed. As the patterns are deviated from more and more, the pulse will tend to be less and less obviously explicated. Such changes are an important source for variations in the rhythm section approach. As noted before, the head is a common place for changing the rhythm section approach, and changes in bass and drum patterns may occur in the head as well as throughout the tune.

Special Patterns

Sometimes a tune will have a special bass line or drum pattern as opposed to one of the standard patterns. This special pattern is often played during the head. *Footprints* has such a bass line (Ex. 7). It is possible to play *Footprints* using that bass line throughout, although a walking bass line is frequently used for the solos. Ben Sidran's version of Miles Davis' *Solar* changes the tune to a great degree by using very specific patterns for the bass and drums for the first four bars of the chorus (Ex. 104).

Ex. 104
Rhythm Section Patterns for *Solar*

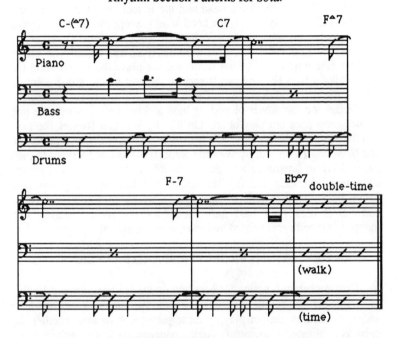

Special patterns may be necessary for tunes that do not fall squarely within the mainstream of the jazz tradition. For example, while *Icarus* by Paul Winter does not use a traditional jazz rhythm section, the tune may be played using nonstandard rhythm section patterns. Because the instrumental roles are different from the standard roles of the jazz rhythm section, the rhythm section must be creative and explore the extent to which the original feel can be duplicated. The closest shorthand label for the rhythm section style used for a tune like *Icarus* would be "straight eighths" (which is not very specific). Ex. 105

shows one possible texture, based closely on recorded versions of *Icarus*.

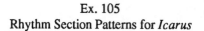

Ex. 105
Rhythm Section Patterns for *Icarus*

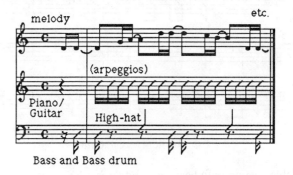

Some contemporary tunes use irregular rhythm section patterns on a consistent basis. In such tunes the bass and drums do not play standard patterns, but improvise an accompaniment in much the same manner as comping instruments do normally. This can be seen in the A section of the head of *April Joy* by Pat Metheny (the B section and solos use more standard patterns). The irregular rhythms in Ex. 106 are loosely based on the first four bars of the second A section of the head in the original recording. A variation of this approach occurs on Metheny's *As Falls Wichita, So Falls Wichita Falls*, in which the pulse is kept not by drums but by arpeggios and rhythmic figures that use straight eighth and sixteenth notes. The pulse is not felt directly, but time is still kept by these rhythms.

Variations on Half-time Feel

The bassist and drummer, independently or in coordination with each other, often vary their standard patterns through the use of different feels. Discussed previously, half-time feel is an important technique that bassists use during the head as a way of contrasting the head and the solos. The drums and piano have some flexibility in how they treat a half-time feel in the head. Generally, their patterns are less dense or may even be at a true half-time feel. The bass is more

Ex. 106
Rhythm Section Patterns for *April Joy*

predictable, stating only beats one and three with occasional fills. The bass may further vary these feels, however, by omitting even more beats from the pattern. For instance, on *Django* by the Modern Jazz Quartet, the bass plays only downbeats and the drums accent the second beat of the first bar and the first beat of the second bar (Ex. 107).

Ex. 107
Bass and Drum Patterns for *Django*

(These accents are derived from the phrasing of the melody.) The head for *Blue Monk* is performed many times with the bass on beat four only, or sometimes on beats four and one.

Pedal Tones

A pedal tone is a constant, single note, usually reiterated by the bass. Sometimes a pedal is composed as part of the tune, as in John

Coltrane's *Naima*. Sometimes it can be added in by the bassist, in which case it usually creates some harmonic tension because the reiterated note clashes with the normal chord changes. It can also add rhythmic interest, as pedals do not need to be played on every beat, but may use any particular rhythmic figure. In the head of *My Favorite Things* by John Coltrane, the bass plays a dominant pedal (a pedal tone on the dominant scale degree) on the A section. *Wave* by Antonio Carlos Jobim uses a tonic pedal in the intro that is also used for the ending vamp.

3/4 Meter

In 3/4 (or waltz-time), bassists will frequently play only one or two notes per bar in order to set up a change to a walking bass line. The straightest (least swinging) feel occurs when these two notes are on beats one and three. A more swinging feel is achieved when these two notes are on beats one and the and-of-two, or the and-of-three. This can be seen in Freddie Hubbard's *Up Jumped Spring* and John Coltrane's version of *My Favorite Things*.

Fills

Filling provides the greatest amount of freedom from standard patterns. When rhythm section members fill for a significant period of time instead of maintaining a standard pattern, the rhythm section approaches collective improvisation. In *Footprints*, as recorded by Dave Liebman, the first chorus of the trumpet solo finds the bass and piano filling, instead of walking or comping (the drums maintain the pulse). The texture becomes much more varied as a result of the spontaneous interaction between the pianist's and the bassist's irregular phrasing and rhythms. *Naima* by John Coltrane demonstrates a high degree of freedom for the bassist and the drummer--their function is merely to fill throughout the tune. The pianist is the time-keeper more than anyone else.

Because the bass and the drums are given the task of explicitly playing the pulse, fills may be very effectively combined with some beat regularly stated. In *Some Day My Prince Will Come*, as recorded by Bobby Hutcherson, the bassist plays on the first beat and freely fills in the remainder of each bar.

Jazz/Rock

It is not uncommon for jazz/rock and funk styles to use a vamp instead of one of the more traditional chorus forms. With a tune based entirely on the vamp, the rhythm section takes a slightly different approach to its standard patterns. The group Weather Report has developed a distinctive style partially based on vamps, with the rhythm section taking the following approach:

1. The drums establish a single pattern and feel, which may be varied or developed.

2. The bass establishes a single pattern, often implying two-, four-, or eight-bar phrases.

3. The keyboard establishes a single chord or tonality (along with the bass) that may be varied; often the harmonic rhythm is very slow, and a feeling of space is achieved by sustained chords or very sparse comping (with frequent, long rests).

4. In coordination with the rhythm section, the saxophone often plays melodies consisting of long, sustained notes with frequent, long rests.

The approach was first established in early Weather Report recordings such as *Second Sunday in August*, *125th Street Congress*, *Will*, *Boogie Woogie Waltz*, *Nubian Sundance*, *American Tango*, and also occurs in many other Weather Report recordings.

Weather Report also favors intros that create a dreamy feeling, are sometimes very short, and lead into a rock or funk style. This feeling, in which rhythm and melody are de-emphasized in favor of tone-color, can be traced back to the first Weather Report LP (*Weather Report*), and can be seen in *Scarlet Woman*, *Mysterious Traveller*, *Elegant People*, *Mr. Gone*, *Gibraltar*, and *Three Clowns*.

Another rhythm section approach to jazz/rock and funk tunes is seen in Jeff Lorber's *Magic Lady*. The drums provide a steady funk time-pattern, but bass and keyboards play a series of predetermined accents and nothing else. This places the rhythm section half-way between playing standard patterns (as do the drums in this example) and only playing accents behind a melody (as do the piano and bass).

Combining Approaches

All the above techniques of varying standard patterns are often alternated or combined. An example in which the drummer uses several different techniques in the head is Bobby Hutcherson's version of *Israel*. In it, the drums play a combination of a normal swing time-pattern, accents that follow the rhythm of the melody, and fills. *Some*

Day My Prince Will Come by Miles Davis uses a varied approach to the bass line. A pedal is used for the intro and is continued into the first eight bars of the head. After that the bassist alternates between merely playing on every downbeat and playing a walking bass line with a note on every pulse. The change from playing downbeats to a walking bass line occurs with a new soloist, or at the beginning of a chorus.

VIII. JAZZ HARMONY

CHORD SYMBOLS

Several different symbols are used for single chords. Preferred symbols are listed before others in Ex. 108. The primary chords of jazz harmony are the 7th chords in Ex. 108 labeled with "*."

Polychord notation is ambiguous in that the letter after the slash ("/") may refer to a chord or a single bass note. The musical context will determine which is appropriate.

RELATIONSHIP BETWEEN CHORDS AND SCALES

Scales and chords are related--a scale can be viewed as a chord laid out horizontally, and a chord can be viewed as a scale stacked vertically. Notes in a scale are labeled with consecutive numbers (1, 2, 3, 4, 5, 6, 7). Notes in a chord are labeled by skipping every other number (1, 3, 5, 7, 9, 11, 13). The basic chords tones are 1, 3, 5, and 7; 9, 11, and 13 are called extensions. Whereas 1, 3, 5, and 7 label both chord tones and scale degrees, the 2, 4, and 6 scale degrees are normally labeled 9, 11, and 13 respectively when considered as part of a chord. Ex. 109 gives the scale, the related chord(s), and possible extensions and alterations for the chord(s) derived from that scale.

Not all possible extensions and alterations derived from scales are used in jazz harmony (for instance, the natural 11 is not used as an extension with major or dominant chords). Among the usable extensions and alterations, any combination is possible when those exten-

Ex. 108
Chord Symbols

Symbol	Name
Triads	
(none) M maj	major triad
- min mi m	minor triad
° dim	diminished triad
+ aug	augmented triad
sus	suspended triad, or sus triad
b5	major triad b5 (rarely used)

Symbol	Name
Sixth Chords	
6 M6 maj6	major sixth chord
-6 min6 mi6 m6	minor sixth chord

Symbol	Name
Seventh Chords	
* Δ7 M7 maj7 7̄	major seventh
+ (Δ7) Δ7(#5)	major seventh #5
Δ7(b5)	major seventh b5 (rarely used)
* 7	dominant seventh
+7 aug7 7(#5)	augmented seventh
7(b5)	dominant seventh b5
* -7 min7 mi7 m7	minor seventh
-7(#5)	minor seventh #5 (rarely used)
-(Δ7) min (Δ7)	minor/major seventh
* ø7 -7(b5)	half-diminished seventh
* °7 dim7	diminished seventh
7sus 7sus4	suspended 4th, or sus 4

Symbol	Name
Polychords	
D/C	polychord (any two chords)
G-7/C G-7/C bass	G-7 chord over a C bass note (equivalent to a C7sus)

Ex. 109
Scales and Related Chords

Ex. 109 (cont'd.)

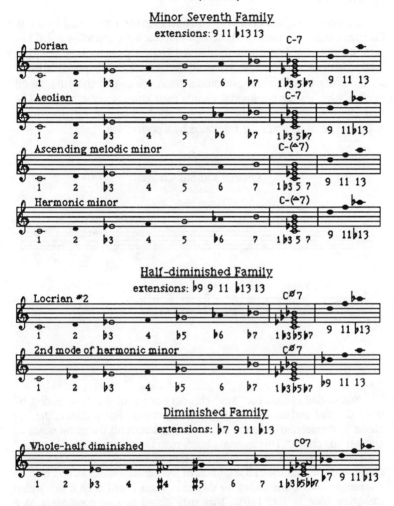

Minor Seventh Family
extensions: 9 11 ♭13 13

Half-diminished Family
extensions: ♭9 9 11 ♭13 13

Diminished Family
extensions: ♭7 9 11 ♭13

sions and alterations are derived from a single scale. Other combinations are possible--the ear is one's best guide. Note that a single chord may have more than one related scale. (The scales are the same ones often used for improvisation.)

Scale degrees and their chromatic alterations are numbered in comparison to the major scale built on the root of the chord.

Quartal and Sus Chords

Quartal chords are chords whose notes are each separated by a 4th. (Tertian chords are chords whose notes are each separated by a 3rd.) In jazz, quartal chords are usually derived from a pentatonic scale. The second measure of Ex. 110 shows all the quartal chords possible using all the notes in a C minor pentatonic scale. Note that the 4ths are all perfect 4ths, giving the quartal chords their characteristic sound. The first chord in the second measure uses all the notes in the pentatonic scale and all of its notes are separated by a perfect 4th.

Ex. 110
Quartal and Sus Chords

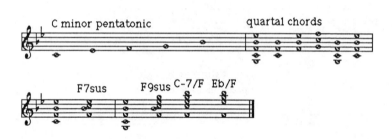

Suspended chords (or "sus" chords) consist of the 1, 4, 5, and b7 scale degrees and are based on quartal harmony. For instance, the last chord in the second measure of Ex. 110 contains all the same notes as another sus chord. This quartal chord, rearranged into a "root position" sus chord, is shown in the third measure of Ex. 110. Another quartal chord, the one that uses all the notes of the pentatonic scale, can also be rearranged into a sus chord, in this case a sus chord with a 9th added (measure four in Ex. 110). This sus9 chord is also equivalent to a widely used polychord (C-7/F in measure four). Both chords contain exactly the same notes. This polychord is sometimes used as a substitute for a dominant function chord, as it consists of a II-7 over a bass note on the dominant scale degree (that is, in Bb major, C-7/F). A variant polychord related to the sus9 chord is created by substituting Eb major for C- over an F bass note (Eb/F, measure four).

NOTATING EXTENSIONS AND ALTERATIONS

A number present outside parentheses denotes itself and all chord tones beneath it--that is, "7" implies the 1, 3, 5, and 7; "11" implies the 1, 3, 5, 7, 9, and 11. Higher extensions without all chord tones beneath it are written inside parentheses--that is, "C△7 (13)" denotes the 1, 3, 5, 7, and 13.

Chromatic alterations (an accidental in a chord symbol) are necessary if the note in question is not a member of the major scale whose tonic is the root of the chord. For instance, the note Bb, as an extension of an F7 chord, is labeled the "11th," and the note B is labeled the "#11" because Bb is diatonic in F major and must be raised a half-step to yield the note B. The "#" does not refer to an actual accidental; it only means that the note is raised a half-step from its diatonic form in the major scale ("b" similarly refers to lowering a note a half-step). All numbers outside parentheses denote chord tones in their diatonic form and do not take accidentals. Numbers are placed inside parentheses before an accidental may be applied. In these cases, a smaller number is then used outside of parentheses: C△7(#9), not C△#9 (Ex. 111).

Ex. 111
Notating Extensions

CHORD PROGRESSIONS AND SUBSTITUTE CHORDS

Strong Root Movement

Certain intervals between the roots of chords will produce a strong harmonic progression. These intervals are:

1. Down a 3rd
2. Up a 2nd
3. Up a perfect 4th

Of these root movement intervals, the strongest is up a perfect 4th. The exact interval for 3rds and 2nds (major 3rd, minor 3rd, major 2nd, minor 2nd) will vary. Jazz harmony favors the root movement up a perfect 4th, and it occurs frequently in the II-V-I progression and in turnarounds. The root movement up a 2nd is usually used in a sequence, such as $I^{\triangle}7$, II-7, III-7, and so on; when VII progresses to I; or when IV is used as a substitute for II progressing to V. The root movement down a 3rd is usually used when I moves to VI, as in a turnaround.

The II-V-I progression is the most common progression in jazz. Often it will appear in a series or cycle. A cycle is any sequence of II-V or II-V-I changes through several different keys with a constant interval between the keys. Common cycles are given below in Ex. 112.

Ex. 112

Cycles

II-V-I down M2:	D-7	G7	$C^{\triangle}7$	C-7	F7	$Bb^{\triangle}7$
II-V up P4:	D-7	G7	G-7	C7	C-7	Bb7
II-V down M2:	D-7	G7	C-7	F7	Bb-7	Eb7
II-V up M2:	D-7	G7	E-7	A7	F#-7	B7
II-V down m2:	D-7	G7	Db-7	Gb7	C-7	F7
II-V up m2:	D-7	G7	Eb-7	Ab7	E-7	A7

Modulation

A modulation to another key may occur at any time, and without preparation, pivot chords, or the like. Jazz depends very much upon such frequent modulations. Ex. 113 is an analysis of modulations in *All the Things You Are*, and illustrates the variety and frequency of modulations in jazz. There are five different keys listed in Ex. 113.

Substitute Chords

Diatonic substitute chords. These may be used when two 7th chords have three notes in common. These substitutions work so well because one of the chords has the same notes as the other chord, but with a higher extension and without a root. For instance, E-7 is a substitute for $C^{\triangle}7$ and has the same notes as a $C^{\triangle}9$ lacking a C root. Ex. 114 lists common diatonic substitutions.

There are always two potential substitute chords for any diatonic chord because the two chords whose roots are a 3rd down and a 3rd up from the root of the original chord will have three notes in common with the original chord. However, not every chord will have two dia-

Ex. 113
Modulations in *All the Things You Are*

A

chords:	F-7	Bb-7	Eb7	Ab△7	Db△7	D-7	G7	C△7
analysis:	VI	II	V	I	IV	II	V	I
keys:	Ab				C			

A

chords:	C-7	F-7	Bb7	Eb△7	Ab△7	A-7	D7	G△7
analysis:	VI	II	V	I	IV	II	V	I
keys:	Eb				G			

B

chords:	A-7	D7	G△7	F#-7	B7	E△7	C+7
analysis:	II	V	I	II	V	I	V/VI
keys:	G			E			Ab

A

chords:	F-7	Bb-7	Eb7	Ab△7	Db△7	Db-7	C-7	Bb7	Bb-7	Eb7	Ab△7
analysis:	VI	II	V	I	IV	IV-	III	V/V	II	V	I
keys:	Ab										

Ex. 114
Diatonic Substitute Chords

chord:	I△7	II-7	III-7	IV△7	V7	VI-7	VII∅7
substitution:	III-7	IV△7	I△7	VI-7	VII∅7	IV△7	V7
	VI-7			II-7		I△7	

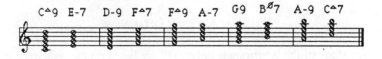

C△9   E-7   D-9   F△7   F△9   A-7   G9   B∅7   A-9   C△7

tonic substitutes. Substitutes for dominant-function chords (V and VII) must have the tritone unique to dominant function chords (between scale degrees 4 and 7). For example, II-7 cannot substitute for VII°7 because it lacks this tritone. Furthermore, diatonic chords with this tritone cannot be substitutes for chords without this tritone. For example, V7 cannot substitute for III-7.

Secondary dominant substitutes. These are dominant-quality chords whose related tonic (that is, the major or minor chord whose root is a perfect 4th above the root of the secondary dominant) is not the first scale degree, but some other diatonic scale degree. This makes a *temporary* tonic of scale degrees other than the first. When used as substitute chords, secondary dominants often progress to this temporary tonic. In Ex. 115 no. 1, D-7 is made a temporary tonic by its secondary dominant, A7. Another common resolution of the secondary dominant is to move to another secondary dominant built on the root of the temporary tonic, making a cycle of secondary dominants. In Ex. 115 no. 2, E7, A7, and D7 are secondary dominants. This progression is often used for the B section of *I Got Rhythm* (usually in Bb major).

Ex. 115
Secondary Dominants

original progression	C$^\triangle$7	A-7	D-7	G7 ‖C$^\triangle$7
1. secondary dominant as substitute	C$^\triangle$7	A7	D-7	G7 ‖C$^\triangle$7
2. cycle of secondary dominants	E7	A7	D7	G7 ‖C$^\triangle$7
3. VII as substitute secondary dominant	C$^\triangle$7	C#^{0}7	D-7	G7 ‖C$^\triangle$7

Tritone substitutes. These are dominant-quality chords used as substitutes for other dominant-quality chords. The interval between the roots of the two chords is a tritone, and the two chords are interchangeable. These chords function extremely well as substitutes because they share the tritone that is essential to dominant-function chords. The 3rd of one chord is the 7th of the other and the 7th of one chord is the 3rd of the other (spelled enharmonically), and all are part of the shared tritone (Ex. 116). Either chord can progress to the other's tonic.

COMMON TURNAROUNDS

Many of the turnarounds in Ex. 117 are based on the principles of chord substitution (others are not derived by the above chord substitution principles, but occur in common practice). The chords labeled "Interchangeable Chords" in Ex. 117 are a group of chords that may be

Ex. 116
Tritone Substitute Chords

G7	C$^{\triangle}$7	=	V7	I (in C)
Db7	C$^{\triangle}$7	=	bII7	I (in C)
G7	F#$^{\triangle}$7	=	bII7	I (in F#)
C#7	F#$^{\triangle}$7	=	V7	I (in F#)

tritone
between roots

G7: $\frac{3}{7}$ Db7: $\frac{7}{3}$

Ex. 117
Turnarounds

Interchangeable Chords

C$^{\triangle}$7	A-7	D-7	G7
E-7	A7	D7	Db7
	Eb7	Ab7	

Other Common Turnarounds

C$^{\triangle}$7		G7	
C$^{\triangle}$7		Db7	
C$^{\triangle}$7		D-7	G7
C$^{\triangle}$7		D-7	Db7
C$^{\triangle}$7	A$^{\emptyset}$7	D7(b9)	G7
C$^{\triangle}$7	A$^{\emptyset}$7	D7(b9)	Db7
C$^{\triangle}$7	A7	D$^{\emptyset}$7	G7(b9)
C$^{\triangle}$7	A-7	D$^{\emptyset}$7	G7(b9)
C$^{\triangle}$7	Eb^{0}7	D-7	G7
C$^{\triangle}$7	Eb^{0}7	D-7	Db7
C$^{\triangle}$7	Eb$^{\triangle}$7	Ab$^{\triangle}$7	Db$^{\triangle}$7
C$^{\triangle}$7	Eb$^{\triangle}$7	Ab$^{\triangle}$7	Db7
C$^{\triangle}$7	Eb7	Ab-7	Db7
C$^{\triangle}$7	F-7	C$^{\triangle}$7	G7
C$^{\triangle}$7	C#^{0}7	D-7	G7

freely substituted for other chords in the same column to produce many different turnarounds.[1]

REHARMONIZING THE GIVEN CHORD PROGRESSION

Any substitution (diatonic, secondary dominant, or tritone) may be made to reharmonize a progression. Changing the chords in a tune for arranging purposes is sometimes necessary, for instance, when the changes as given in a lead sheet or fake book are either incorrect, too complicated, or misleading.

Seventh Chords Instead of Triads or Sixth Chords

In general, mainstream jazz does not use triads. Chords that should be 7th chords and are notated as triads most often occur in older lead sheets or fake books. In some styles, such as jazz/rock and other contemporary styles, a triad may be specifically called for by the composer. The musical context should determine whether or not substituting the 7th chord for the triad is appropriate.

Major chords. In a swing tune in which the progression G7 C occurs, the C chord should be a $C^{\Delta}7$ (another alternative popular in older styles is C6).

Augmented chords. Similarly, augmented triads should be changed to either a $^{\Delta}7(\#5)$ or a +7 chord, depending on the harmonic context. In the progression C+ $F^{\Delta}7$, the C+ should be changed to C+7; in the progression $C^{\Delta}7$ C+ $C^{\Delta}7$, the C+ should be changed to $C^{\Delta}7(\#5)$.

Half-diminished chords. A half-diminished chord should be used instead of a minor sixth chord when it progresses to a dominant chord a whole step up ($D^{\emptyset}7$ G7 and not F-6 G7).

Diminished chords. The diminished 7th chord presents a special case for substitutions, because they are sometimes notated with the wrong root. Because the interval between every two adjacent chord tones is the same (a minor 3rd) any chord tone of a diminished 7th chord may be considered to be the root of another substitute diminished 7th chord with exactly the same chord tones. For example, a $C^{o}7$ chord has exactly the same chord tones as the diminished seventh

---

[1] For more chord progression variations, see Billy Taylor's article on chord substitution for *I Got Rhythm*, and David Baker's set of chord variations for the blues (Billy Taylor, "Jazz Improvisation: 'Rhythm Changes," *Contemporary Keyboard*, October 1977, p. 59; David Baker, *Jazz Improvisation: A Comprehensive Method of Study for All Players*, rev. ed. (Bloomington, Indiana: Frangipani Press, 1983), pp. 70-71).

chords whose roots are chord tones of a C^o7 chord ($C^o7 = Eb^o7 = Gb^o7 = A^o7$, Ex. 118).

Ex. 118
Diminished Chords

$$C^o7 = Eb^o7 = Gb^o7 = A^o7$$

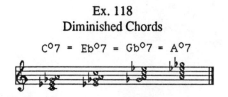

The root of a diminished chord should be chosen so that the diminished chord can be analyzed as a VII chord, or as a VII secondary dominant. This is illustrated in Ex. 119.

Ex. 119
Root Substitutions in Diminished Chords

original:	Bb7	D^o7	C-7	F7

substitution:	Bb7	B^o7	C-7	F7
	I	VII/II	II	V

Cycles

Cycles are rarely necessary to reharmonize a progression, but can be used for variety. In using cycles to reharmonize a progression, a target chord must be chosen. A target chord is usually a tonic chord appearing near the end of a phrase that can be preceded by a cycle reharmonization. Once the potential target chord is identified, a cycle is introduced into the progression by working backwards from the target chord. In the progression F#-7 B7 E-7 A7 D-7 G7 C△7, the tonic chord C△7 is first preceded by a II-V, which is then preceded by another II-V, and so on, creating a cycle leading up to the target chord. Any cycle (or combination of II-V or II-V-I progressions in any keys) may be used. In every case, however, the reharmonized chords must agree with the given melody. In general, this means that every melody note must be capable of being analyzed as either a chord tone, an extension/alteration appropriate to that quality chord, or as part of a related scale.

IX. HARMONIZATION
AND ORCHESTRATION

There are two arranging techniques that fall under the broad category of harmonization:

1. Assigning one, two, or three instruments to play a given melody in which the added parts duplicate exactly the rhythm of the given melody (note-to-note harmonization)[1]

2. Adding a background or counterpoint to a given melody, in which the added parts do not duplicate the rhythm of the given melody

Assigning new chords to a given melody is reharmonization (see pages 96-97).

When using the following methods to harmonize a given melody, flexibility is required. A composer has the option of conceiving of a melody and its harmonization at the same time, and this means that a particular harmonization technique may be applied more consistently. It may be that a given melody lends itself very well to one particular harmonization technique. But it may also very well happen that a given melody will *not* lend itself to one particular technique. Techniques may be alternated as required by the given melody. When in doubt, rely on the sound--play it or sing it.

---

[1] Four-part harmonization is beyond the scope of this book and has been well covered in many arranging books that emphasize big band arranging (see Bibliography).

ONE-PART WRITING

One-part writing means that there is only one melody to orchestrate.

One Instrument Playing the Entire Melody

This is the easiest and simplest option. A different instrument may play the melody at the end of the tune than at the beginning, or upon a repetition of the melody. In one version of Thelonious Monk's *Straight No Chaser* Monk plays the first head, and then vibes and sax play the head the second time.

Unison and Octave Doubling

Two or more instruments may play a melody at the unison or at any octave. In jazz/rock, a very common technique involves several instruments playing a syncopated melody in unison, as in Ex. 120.

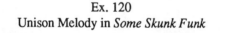

Ex. 120
Unison Melody in *Some Skunk Funk*

℗ & © 1975 Arista Records, Inc.

Dividing the Melody into Phrases

With more than one melody instrument, the melody can be divided into smaller phrases and each phrase assigned to different instruments. This may be done frequently for every possible fragment of the melody, or relatively infrequently. Ex. 121 illustrates a very frequent division of the melody in *Straight No Chaser*. The most common format for infrequent changing among instruments is illustrated in AABA tunes. The A sections are played by one instrument, and the B section is played by another.

While not strictly a one-part technique, overlapping adjacent phrases is often done. This technique divides the melody into smaller

Ex. 121
Divided Melody for *Straight No Chaser*

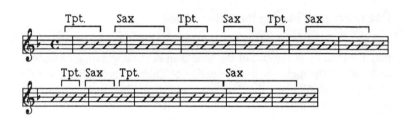

Ex. 122
Overlapping Phrases

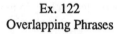

phrases. The last note of a phrase is sustained while a new instrument begins the next phrase (Ex. 122). This gives a smooth flow to the harmonization and prevents a choppy feel. The harmonization works best when the phrase ends on a chord tone so that the changes are well defined.

TWO-PART WRITING,
NOTE-TO-NOTE

Two-part writing uses two instruments simultaneously. In any of the two- or three-part techniques discussed, other instruments can double one part at the unison or the octave. Two-part writing refers not to the total number of instruments playing, but to the number of different melodic lines, any of which may be doubled as in one-part writing.

Parallel Writing

In parallel harmonization, one instrument plays the melody and the other instrument harmonizes the melody at an interval that remains constant. The contour and the rhythm of both lines are exactly the same--they merely start on a different note. The melody part may be either above or below the harmonization, although it is usually below.

The particular style of jazz sometimes determines the interval separating the two parts. For most mainstream jazz tunes with common II-V-I progressions, the most commonly used intervals are 3rds and 6ths, which produce a very consonant effect. These 3rds and 6ths are not strictly parallel, but are diatonic. This means that the note for the harmonization is selected from the related tonic scale, and therefore some 3rds and 6ths will be major and others minor (Ex. 123).

Ex. 123
Harmonization in 3rds

(The D# in the lower part of Ex. 123 is not a diatonic harmonization, but is part of a strict parallel movement in minor 3rds used to harmonize the F# chromatic passing tone.) Because the tune will most likely move through several different keys, the related tonic scale will change. Ex. 124 is a harmonization of *Blue Monk* using 3rds and 6ths.

Most modal or pentatonic-based tunes, such as *Footprints*, use 4ths or 5ths (Ex. 125). They may be either strictly parallel (as in Ex. 125) or diatonic. Also appropriate for this style are 3rds and 6ths.

The dissonant intervals (2nds and 7ths) are rarely used. They are, however, stylistically appropriate for free or atonal styles. No more glaring example of harmonization in 2nds can be found than the sustained notes at the ends of short phrases in Oliver Lake's version of Eric Dolphy's *The Prophet*. Charles Mingus' version of *Ladybird* (see page 42) uses minor 2nds to harmonize most of the melody.

Ex. 124
Harmonization for *Blue Monk*

Ex. 125
Harmonization for *Footprints*

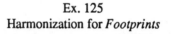

A related technique is bitonal harmonization. By keeping an interval absolutely constant between two voices, each voice, in effect, plays its melody in a different key. George Russell uses this in his version of *Au Privave*.

Nonparallel Writing

There are two methods of note-to-note harmonization in which the intervals between the two parts change. The harmonization notes are chosen on the basis of how well the combination of the harmonization and the original melody defines the given chord. Contrary and oblique motion, as well as similar motion (parallel writing), may be used.

1. The first kind of nonparallel, note-to-note writing works best for sections of melodies that contain only chord tones (such as the A section of *All the Things You Are*). The predominant intervals are 3rds and 6ths, and the 3rd or the 7th of the chord (or both) should be present (Ex. 126).

Ex. 126
Nonparallel Harmonization #1

2. In another method, a single chord tone (often the 3rd or the 7th) that the melody does not contain is chosen and is given the rhythm of the melody (Ex. 127). The intervals between the two parts will be constantly changing. Chord tones common between two chords are often repeated (for example, the Eb in the harmonization of the C-7 in Ex. 127 is repeated for F7). This technique can be used easily in a head arrangement without needing a written part.

Ex. 127
Nonparallel Harmonization #2

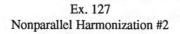

THREE-PART WRITING,
NOTE-TO-NOTE

In three-part harmonization, the quality of the given 7th chord and whether the given melody note is a chord tone, an extension, or neither determines the harmonization. In general, the harmonization should conform to the following principles:

Span one octave or less
Add two parts below the given melody
Do not double (repeat) any note in two voices
Do not have a half-step between the upper two voices
Include as much parallel motion as possible

The first two principles below are the main guides for adding two parts in a three-part harmonization:

1. Add the 3rd and the 7th to the given note. If the given note is the 3rd or the 7th, add the other one (the 7th or the 3rd) and any other chord tone. If the melody note is an appropriate higher extension, the 3rd or the 7th may be added along with another chord tone.

2. If the melody note is the 1st, 3rd, or 5th, a triad may be used (harmonizations using the 3rd and the 7th are preferred).

The following are exceptions to the first two principles:

3. The 5th of a major or minor triad may be changed to the 6th (making a major or minor sixth chord) when using triads to harmonize major and minor 7th chords.

4. For $^{\phi}7$ chords, the harmonization should include the b5, avoiding major 2nds between the upper two voices.

5. For $^{o}7$ chords, add any two other chord tones to the given note.

6. For $^{\Delta}7$ and -7 chords, the 5th and the 3rd may be added to a given 9 or b9.

7. If a given melody note to be harmonized is not a chord tone or an appropriate extension (for instance, a #11 with a minor 7 chord), it should be harmonized exactly parallel to the harmonization for the next melody note.

A complete list of three-part voicings is given in Ex. 128. The above principles are applied to an actual melody in Ex. 129. The number in the above paragraphs for each principle is given below each harmonized chord in Ex. 129 that uses that principle.

Ex. 128
Three-part Voicings

Ex. 129
Three-part Harmonization

Diatonic Triads

Another option for a three-part harmonization is to use only paral-lel diatonic triads. This technique works best when the entire melody or section of a melody is diatonic. Because most jazz tunes change key frequently, the key that provides these diatonic chords may change often. A diatonic melody note may be considered as either the root, 3rd, or 5th of any diatonic triad, and harmonized as such. Major and minor triads are normally used; diminished and augmented triads are used sparingly. Each subsequent note is harmonized with parallel triads in the same inversion (Ex. 130). A series of triads may change inversion, in which case they will not be parallel.

Ex. 130
Diatonic Triad Harmonization

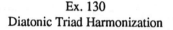

Quartal Voicings

Quartal chords (that is, chords based on the interval of a 4th, and especially the perfect 4th) are often used to harmonize modal or pentatonic-based tunes, but can also be used to harmonize tonal II-V-I tunes.

Quartal voicings can be very effective for the II-V-I progression. Because these voicings are not tertian voicings, the principle that the 3rd and 7th best define the chord is relaxed (except for dominant chords). Instead, any voicing that is compatible with the quality of the chord can be used. One important distinction, therefore, is whether a voicing has a tritone or not: voicings with tritones are normally used for dominant-function chords, and not for nondominant-function chords. Preferred voicings are given in Ex. 131.

Quartal voicings are frequently used to harmonize minor 7th chords in modal tunes. These quartal voicings can be either strictly parallel or diatonic to the mode. If diatonic, some voicings will contain a tritone and not consist solely of perfect 4ths (Ex. 132). The decision

Ex. 131
Quartal Voicings (II-V-I)

Ex. 132
Quartal Voicings (Dorian)

to use diatonic or parallel quartal voicings depends on whether the special quality of perfect 4th quartal chords is desired.

Polychords

Three-part polychord harmonization involves harmonizing a note with a triad that is derived by making a polychord out of extensions and alterations to the given chord. As certain quality chords take certain extensions and alterations, only some polychords will work for specific chords. Ex. 133 lists possible polychords for major, dominant, minor, and half-diminished chords. Only major and minor polychords derived from extensions are listed.

SPACINGS AND INVERSIONS

Any of the above harmonization techniques may be written in two spacings: open or close position. Close position means that there is less than an octave between the highest and lowest note of the voicing; open position means that there is more than an octave between the highest and lowest note of the voicing. Open position is easily achieved by taking a close-position chord and dropping the second voice down an octave (Ex. 134).

Another principle of voicing related to open position is the

Ex. 133
Polychords

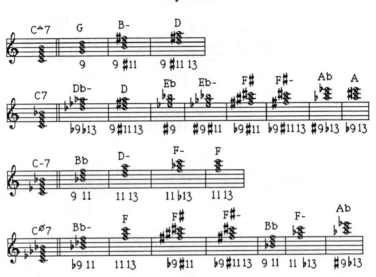

Ex. 134
Open and Close Positions

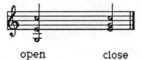

open   close

principle that wider intervals should occur at lower ranges. Very small intervals, such as 2nds and 3rds, tend to blur at low ranges.

Any of the above harmonization techniques may also be used in root position or in any inversion.

COMBINATIONS OF INSTRUMENTS

The primary principle in combining instruments is that an instrument playing in its practical, comfortable range will be able to produce its sound and tone better, thus ensuring a basic equality among the combined instruments. Consequently, the effective range for a particular combination is limited to the area which is comfortable for *both* instruments. This also means that doublings greater than an octave are possible, such as at the 10th or the 13th, but doubling at two octaves is rare. While a contrapuntal combination of instruments will allow each part to be heard more easily than a note-to-note combination, the consideration of the comfortable, practical range of the instruments is primary in both cases. See Appendix B for practical and overall ranges of instruments.

Conversely, combining instruments such that one of them is in an uncomfortable or extreme part of its range will often not achieve a good blend. Either the instrument will dominate the blend, or will be covered up by another instrument. For instance, a flute in its lowest octave will tend to be absorbed by most combinations. This may be compensated to a limited degree by increasing its volume.[2]

LIMITED HARMONIZATION

Not every melody note needs to be harmonized, as is done in note-to-note harmonization. Accents that the rhythm section might play, or beginnings and ends of phrases are likely places where a limited note-to-note harmonization can take place (Ex. 135). This can be used with any number of parts (one-, two-, or three-part writing).

Ex. 135
Limited Harmonization

---

[2]For a list evaluating combinations of instruments, see William Russo's *Composing for the Jazz Orchestra* (Chicago: University of Chicago Press, 1961), pp.65-78.

COUNTERPOINT AND BACKGROUNDS

As opposed to a note-to-note harmonization, counterpoint and backgrounds have a different rhythm than that of the original melody. Backgrounds imply less activity or movement, and are therefore secondary melodies of less importance than the original melody. Counterpoint implies a level of activity of equal importance to the original melody.

Guide-tone Backgrounds

With a total of two parts, one part may take the melody and the other may take a background part. Backgrounds are usually smooth and unobtrusive, being less important than the original melody. The basic technique involves sustaining a chord tone for the duration of a chord, and moving as smoothly as possible to a chord tone in the next chord (preferably by step or by sustaining a common chord tone between the two chords). This is most easily done by initially choosing the 3rd or 7th of a chord, which also adds further definition to the chord progression. These notes are sometimes called guide-tones. This technique is almost the same as the harmonization technique in which a chord tone is repeated using the rhythm of the melody except that the guide-tone background is usually sustained and not rhythmic, and 3rds and 7ths are used exclusively. In a II-V-I progression or any progression that uses the root movement of up a 4th, the 3rd or the 7th will become a chord tone of the next chord and will either be sustained or will move down a step to the 7th (if it was the 3rd) or to the 3rd (if it was the 7th) of the next chord (Ex. 136).

With three parts, the background can take two, leaving one for the original melody. In this case, the two-part background should still define the changes as well as possible. Chord tones should be used, and at least one 3rd or 7th should be included. The melody note should generally not be doubled. A very exact definition of the changes is achieved if both the 3rd and 7th are included in the background. In order to provide some variety to the texture of the background, short notes may be substituted for long, sustained notes. Also, adding a rhythm to the harmonization by repeating it (usually in a syncopated fashion) can add rhythmic variety to the background. Ex. 136 shows all these guide-tone backgrounds for the same melody.

While appearing much the same as a guide-tone background, the background in Charles Mingus' version of *All the Things You Are* (entitled *All the Things You Can C Sharp*) uses only a few true guide-tones (Ex. 137). It is based on a motive from the intro (see Ex. 18).

Ex. 136
Guide-tone Backgrounds

Ex. 137
Background for *All the Things You Can C Sharp*
(*All the Things You Are*)

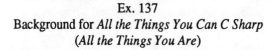

The variety possible with backgrounds of all kinds can be gradually expanded to create a background that is almost as active and as important as the original melody. The rhythms and phrasing of the accents used for *Blue Train* (Ex. 100) are appropriate for backgrounds and may be harmonized by the rhythm section or by wind instruments.

Melodically-oriented Backgrounds

A primary function of guide-tones is to delineate the harmony. Backgrounds also may be more melodically oriented. Riffs are often used as backgrounds during the last choruses of a solo, and are easily created and learned on the spot. Hank Mobley used an interlude that Dizzy Gillespie added to Bud Powell's *52nd Street Theme* as the head for the tune, and used Powell's original head (a riff repeated three times) as a background for the last A section of the solos.

Counterpoint

There are several different textures that counterpoint frequently uses. They are derived from harmonization techniques previously discussed and are harmonized in a similar manner. It is not uncommon for all these textures to appear in any one example of counterpoint (illustrated in Ex. 138).

1. The first texture is an overlap between two melodies, similar to the overlap between phrases when assigning different instruments to an original melody (see pages 99-100). In this texture, the phrasing of the two melodies is complementary, that is, one is active while the other is resting or less active. The counterpoint to the given melody is active when the given melody is sustaining a note or resting. The less active voice is frequently a guide-tone. As with the guide-tone background, the clearest definition of the changes is achieved when the sustained note is the 3rd or the 7th of the chord.

2. A second texture relies on a note-to-note harmonization of the original melody. Because the melodic aspect is emphasized in counterpoint, there is somewhat less of a need for the harmonization to define the chord progression. Contrary motion and oblique motion help to emphasize the independence of the two parts. However, if carried on too long, this note-to-note harmonization becomes just that and not counterpoint. In Ex. 138,

Ex. 138
Counterpoint

a note-to-note harmonization lasts only for two or three successive notes at a time.

3. The third texture involves differing time-values between two simultaneous melodies without complementary phrasing as in the first texture discussed above. In this case, longer time-values are harmonized on the same principles as are backgrounds, the structure and the texture of the two being basically the same.

Instead of a newly composed contrapuntal line, counterpoint can be derived from the melody of the head. In *Bag's Groove* by the Modern Jazz Quartet, the piano is in imitative counterpoint with the melody (Ex. 139). While the vibes play the melody, the piano copies the first two notes of the melody two beats after the vibes, and fills the rest of each four-bar phrase. Miles Davis' version of *Well You Needn't*

Ex. 139
Counterpoint for *Bag's Groove*

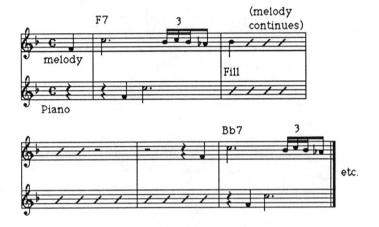

uses an ingenious delay and switching of imitative counterpoint (Ex. 140). In Ex. 140, lines are drawn between each phrase of the original melody and its delayed imitation in the counterpoint. David Murray's *Blues in the Pocket* uses the main melodic line from the head as a counterpoint to the first solo.

The version of *Bag's Groove* by the Modern Jazz Quartet previously cited continues exploring counterpoint during the vibes solo. The piano, instead of comping, improvises relatively simple, riff-like lines behind the vibes solo. Even though both vibes and piano are improvising, the piano is secondary to the vibes.

A relatively rare arranging technique is that of playing two different heads simultaneously. In the case of Dewey Redman's version of *Half Nelson*, the piano plays a harmonization of the melody to *Ladybird* by Tadd Dameron, the tune on which the changes of *Half Nelson* are based (Ex. 141). This harmonization functions as a contrapuntal background line to the melody of *Half Nelson* as well as a comping figure for the piano. In his arrangement of *Tea for Two*, Charles Mingus includes the melody of *Perdido* as a counterpoint to the melody

Ex. 140
Counterpoint for *Well You Needn't*

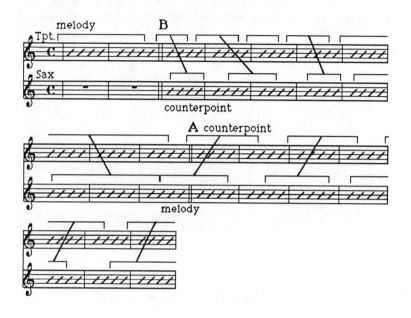

Ex. 141
Two Heads: *Half Nelson* and *Ladybird*

of *Tea for Two* for the first eight bars, and the melody of *Body and Soul* as counterpoint for the next eight bars (Ex. 142). The changes of *Perdido*, *Tea for Two*, and *Body and Soul* stay basically within one key throughout the A sections, so all melodies remain diatonic and essentially consonant.

Ex. 142
Two Heads: *Tea for Two* and *Perdido*

NEW MELODIES

New melodies (composed by an arranger and not by the original composer of the tune) not accompanied by an improvised solo or other counterpoint are not very common. No doubt to highlight his vocal conception and technique, Mark Murphy's version of *Stolen Moments* includes such a line, harmonized as well as performed in unison by Murphy and the horns. Even though this line is improvisatory (it sounds like an improvised line), it was composed and no doubt learned as such by the performers.

Ex. 143
New Melody for *Stolen Moments*

APPENDIX A - NOTATION

SLASHES

Slashes stand for successive beats within a bar, and imply that the rhythm section is performing its standard function (i.e., chordal instruments accompany, bass plays a stylistically appropriate bass line, drums play a time-pattern). For melodic instruments, slashes imply an improvised solo (Ex. 144).

Ex. 144
Slashes

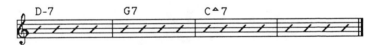

RHYTHMS WITHOUT PITCH

Notes with oversized note-heads are used to notate rhythms performed by the rhythm section. This notation is sufficient when specific notes, voicings, or parts of the drum set need not be specified. When rhythms with specific voicings or notes are required, a single pitch (usually the top note of the voicing) with chord symbols will suffice.

The notation in Ex. 145 indicates that the drummer should not maintain a standard time-pattern while playing the notated rhythm. In order to indicate a rhythm that should be *added* to a standard time-pattern, the following notation should be used (Ex. 146). Note that a specific part of the drum set, such as the high-hat, may be called for. If no abbreviation is used, the drummer decides which part of the set to use. If a complete pattern is to be notated, then each part of the drum set is given a space on the staff.

Ex. 145
Rhythms Without Pitch

Ex. 146
Rhythms Added to Standard Pattern

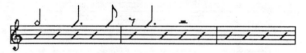

DOUBLE BAR

The double bar is used to delineate major sections within the form of a tune (eight-bar phrases, intros, endings, tempo and feel changes, etc.) and may be used liberally (Ex. 147).

Ex. 147
Double Bar

ARTICULATIONS

Ex. 148
Articulations

Ex. 148 (cont'd.)

APPENDIX B - INSTRUMENTATION

TRANSPOSITION

Some instruments are transposing instruments, which means that the pitch that is heard is different from the one read by the performer on the performer's music. The interval between the pitch that the performer reads and the pitch that sounds is called the transposition interval. The transposition interval is accompanied by a direction (up or down) one must move going *from* the sounding pitch *to* the written pitch. For example, moving from the pitch the trumpet sounds to the pitch the performer reads, one would move *up* a major 2nd. The transposition interval for the trumpet is therefore up a major 2nd. Instruments are said to be "in" a key (for example, a trumpet is "in" Bb, and hence the name "Bb trumpet"). The transposition interval is also the interval between the pitch C and the note that signifies what key an instrument is "in." Moving from the note that signifies what key an instrument is in by the amount and in the direction of the transposition interval, one will always arrive at the pitch C. For the Bb trumpet, moving up a major 2nd (the trumpet's transposition interval and direction) from Bb, one arrives at the pitch C. Also, the transposition interval can be used to transpose key signatures in a similar manner. For instance, if the Bb trumpet is to play in the sounding key of F, then the written part should use the key signature a major 2nd higher, that of G.

The key in which transposing instruments sound and in which non-transposing instruments both sound and read is called the "concert" key. Non-transposing instruments are always in C (or "concert" key), and their written and sounding pitches are the same.

RANGES

Written, sounding, complete, and practical ranges, as well as the keys that instruments are in and their transposition intervals are given in Ex. 149.

Written range. The range of the instrument in terms of the notation the performer reads.

Sounding range. The range of the instrument as it is actually heard (in concert key). This is the same as the written range for nontransposing instruments.

Complete range. The entire range of notes possible on an instrument without special techniques or heroic efforts. This is notated in Ex. 149 by whole notes.

Practical range. The range suggested for most arranging situations; in general this range omits notes that are more difficult to produce. Of course, many performers will be able to go beyond this practical range. This is notated in Ex. 149 by filled-in note-heads.

Ex. 149
Ranges and Transpositions

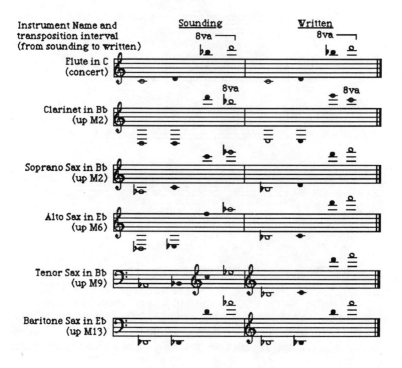

Ex. 149 (cont'd.)

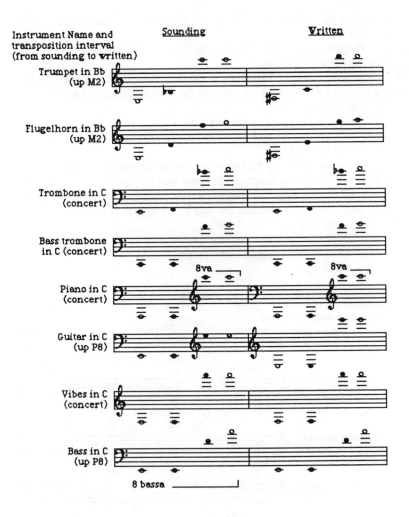

BRASS MUTES

All mutes change the tone-color of an instrument and at the same
time lessen the volume of the instrument. Mutes should be used with
several cautions in mind: technical difficulties increase with the use of
mutes; high and low registers are generally more difficult to negotiate;

fast passages are harder; good intonation is more difficult. Time must be allotted in an arrangement for a performer to put on the mute (at least five seconds) or remove it (only a couple of seconds).

Types of Brass Mutes

Straight Mute
>Sharp, biting edge; narrow tone
>Oriented toward percussive rather than sustained or legato
>>passages
>Does not blend as well as other mutes
>Difficult on trombone

Cup Mute
>Light tone, soft and mellow
>Blends well

Harmon Mute
>Sharp and penetrating tone, but a distant and filtered sound
>More metallic tone than the straight mute, most distinctive tone of
>>all mutes
>Middle and high registers characteristic, lowest octave difficult
>Sustained and legato passages characteristic
>For trumpet only

Bucket Mute
>Soft, muffled, and very mellow tone
>Blends very well

Hat
>Hollow, remote tone
>Rounds out the tone, reducing edge and piercing qualities
>Substitute--"in stand" or "hand over bell"

Plunger Mute
>Deadens sound drastically
>Normally used open and closed (wa-wa effect)
>The business end of a plumber's helper[1]

---

[1]Do not go into a hardware store and ask to buy only the rubber end of a plumber's helper!

APPENDIX C
THE RHYTHM SECTION

COMPING

Comping means accompanying a soloist and providing a chordal background. The primary task is to complement and support the soloist, and to musically suggest ideas to the group and the soloist.

Listening to excellent jazz musicians comp is essential in order to achieve a good feel for comping rhythms. Jazz rhythm is usually very syncopated, emphasizing the offbeats. In addition, the following outlines some typical rhythms used in comping:

1. Any single offbeat

2. Any combination of offbeats, such as successive or alternating

3. Any rhythm on the beat, followed or preceded by rhythm on any offbeat--at most no more than two chords in succession on the beat (Ex. 150)[1]

The examples in Ex. 150 may be played with any combination of long or short articulations.

Straight eighth note styles (that is, styles that do not use swing eighth notes, such as Latin, rock, etc.) have a slight tendency to use less syncopated rhythms and to emphasize the pulse. Often, there is little difference between comping rhythms in different styles. One exception

---

[1]For a transcription of comping rhythms as well as voicings, see Jamey Aebersold's *Transcribed Piano Voicings: Comping to the Record "A New Approach to Jazz Improvisation, vol. 1"* (New Albany: Jamey Aebersold, 1980).

Ex. 150
Comping Rhythms

to this is the ballad style. Ballads require a nonpercussive orientation. Sustained chords occur much more frequently than in other styles.

Comping must strike a balance between activity and inactivity. Often, inexperienced players will comp too frequently, not leaving enough rests and not letting the phrasing breathe. Of course, experienced players will be able to make a busy comping style work effectively.

If there are two comping instruments in a group, the players must develop a way to stay out of each other's way while comping. A common problem occurs when both comping instruments are so busy that the chordal background becomes muddled. There are several solutions to this problem. One solution is to have only one comping instrument play at a time--the two can trade comping chores every chorus, every soloist, every tune, or at any rate. With experienced players, both comping instruments can play at the same time. Generally, each becomes much less busy and active than when comping alone in order to leave room for the other comping instrument. The principle of counterpoint applies in this case: while one is busy, the other should not be so busy.

Piano chord voicings are based on the following principles:

1. The basic voicing is a three- or four-note voicing played by the left hand within an octave either side of middle C.

2. The bottom note of the voicing should be the 3rd or 7th of the chord; this means that roots are not played by piano or guitar (they are played by the bass player).

3. Chords are usually connected in as smooth a manner as possible.

4. The pedal is not used except on ballads.

Basic voicings for the five main jazz chords as well as the II-V-I progression in a major and a minor key are given in Ex. 151.

Ex. 151
Piano Voicings

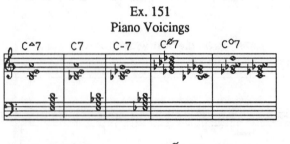

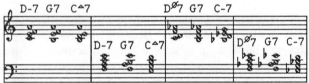

Comping instruments also have the option of introducing substitute chord progressions during their comping. Many times diatonic and tritone substitutions can be introduced at will by the comping instruments without conflicting with a soloist or the melody. Chords that are diatonically or chromatically parallel to the given chord may also be freely introduced (Ex. 152). However, the particular set of extensions and alterations to a chord must fit those implied by the melody and by the soloist. If a soloist plays a b13, for example, and the comping instrument plays a natural 13, a harmonic conflict will result. It may be necessary to discuss the exact extensions being used. The goal for each member is to be able to hear which extensions are being used and automatically adjust their voicings or solo line. With sensitive players, a comping instrument can sometimes introduce radically different

Ex. 152
Passing Chords

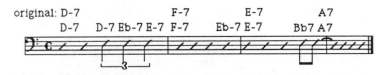

original: D-7   F-7   E-7   A7
    D-7   D-7 Eb-7 E-7 F-7   Eb-7 E-7   Bb7 A7

changes into a progression. An example of this occurs on Pat Martino's version of *Blue Bossa* in which the pianist plays free parallel chords for the first eight bars of the fourth and fifth solo choruses and a two-chord vamp for the first eight bars of the sixth solo chorus. The tension built up by these dissonant chords is released in the second eight bars of each chorus.

BASS LINES

Walking Bass Lines

Walking bass lines are composed of scales, chord arpeggios, and approach tones. In general, certain chord tones occur more frequently and on certain beats. These tendencies are listed in Ex. 153.

Ex. 153
Constructing a Walking Bass Line

Beat 1   root
Beat 2   3rd, 5th, or 7th
Beat 3   3rd, 5th, or 7th
Beat 4   any chord tone; approach tones

Bass lines may also consist of scale passages. Even when using scale passages in a bass line, the first beat of a new chord will still tend to take the chord root. Arpeggios and scale passages should be balanced in a bass line.

These principles of bass line construction are illustrated in Ex. 154. The basic rhythm for a walking bass line is to state every beat. For rhythmic variety, eighth notes between beats may be inserted occasionally, often as diatonic or chromatic neighbors, approached by leap and left by step. A principle of melody construction in general as well as bass line construction states that the larger the skip, the greater the

tendency for the next interval to be stepwise in the opposite direction. This is illustrated at the points marked "*" in Ex. 154.

Ex. 154
Sample Walking Bass Line

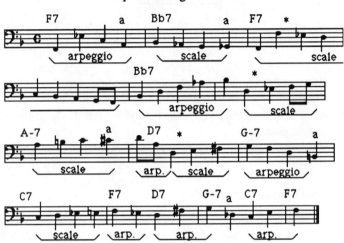

a = approach tone
* = return in opposite direction after large skip

Latin Bass Lines

Sample Latin bass lines are shown in Ex. 155. The rhythmic patterns of these bass lines give them their Latin flavor. Many variations of these bass lines are possible. Also, it should be noted that roots and 5ths predominate in Latin bass lines more than in walking bass lines.

Ex. 155
Latin Bass Lines

TIME-PATTERNS FOR DRUMS

Ex. 156 is a list of standard time-patterns for drums for various styles of jazz. Many variations are widely used--the patterns illustrated should be taken as starting points.

Ex. 156
Standard Time-patterns

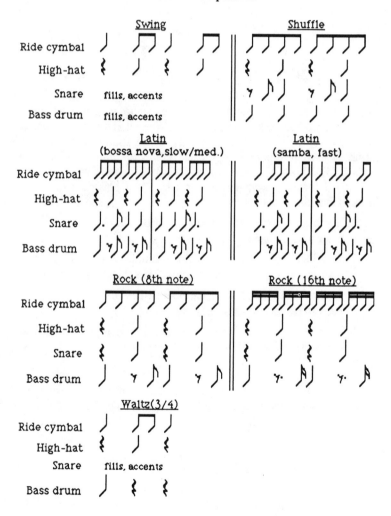

APPENDIX D
ANNOTATED ARRANGEMENT

This annotated arrangement illustrates some arranging techniques in one complete arrangement (Ex. 158). While it is often not necessary to completely write out an arrangement in the following manner, this format is used in order to show exactly how an entire tune might be performed. The head chart is also included for reference (Ex. 157). The actual form an arrangement can take when presented to the performers in a group can vary widely.

1. Some arrangements need not be written at all, but merely discussed beforehand.

2. A written arrangment may include as little as the head chart with instructions ("no intro, head, solos, fours, head, vamp & fade").

3. Unless backgrounds and harmonizations are improvised, they need to be notated as well.

4. A written arrangement may include as much as every bar and note notated, much like nonimprovised music.

Intro

The intro is a four-bar turnaround based on the first two chords of the head, is stated twice, and includes a trumpet solo. The G-7 and F#7 chords do not come from the head, but merely move back to the tonic F△7.

Breaks

The break at the beginning of every A section in the head is somewhat unusual in that it occurs in the first bar of the head, and not in the bar directly before the first A section, as is normal.

In the solo break before the solo section, the soloist may improvise over the $F^\triangle 7$ chord or over a turnaround of the soloist's choosing.

Rhythm Section Accents

The break at the beginning of every A section in the head is preceded and followed by short accents from the rhythm section. These accents help emphasize the break. The two accents in the first bar of the head outline the melody at that point. The accent at the beginning of the B section helps delineate the form of the tune as well as highlight the melody. The accents before the solo break perform a similar function, but create somewhat more tension because there are relatively many accents in a short period of time. This tension is released in the solo break and the beginning of the following solo.

Harmonization

The melody during the head is both harmonized and divided among the three melody instruments. The trumpet plays most of the melody by itself. In the first two bars of each A section, the sax and trombone harmonize the trumpet melody. In the last four bars of the A section, the melody is divided into short phrases, alternating between the trumpet and the alto sax. This also occurs in bars 5 and 6 of the last A section. Each short phrase overlaps the next one by sustaining the last note of the phrase. The B section harmonizes the melody in unison until the bar before the next A section. The last three notes of the melody in the last A section are harmonized through the use of parallel triads.

The backgrounds for the solos are harmonized in unison using guide-tones and are given a simple rhythm. If a wind instrument solos, either or both of the other two may play the background. Note that the backgrounds are not continuous, but include frequent rests for the soloist.

Solos

The solo order, as well as the number of choruses for each soloist, is not indicated--it therefore needs to be worked out beforehand or through visual cues.

Fours

One chorus of fours is indicated in the score. During the last four bars of the section of fours, the drummer should play the accent on the and-of-four (which also occurrs immediately before the first downbeat of the head) in order to set up the break that begins the head.

Ending

The ending at the notation "fine" is an accented, staccato ending.

Ex. 157
Head Chart for *Rest-stop*

Ex. 158
Annotated Arrangement for *Rest-stop*

Rest-stop

by Paul Rinzler

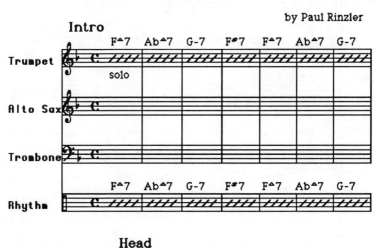

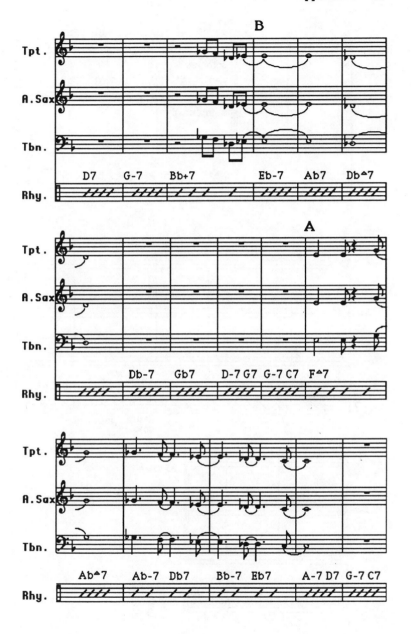

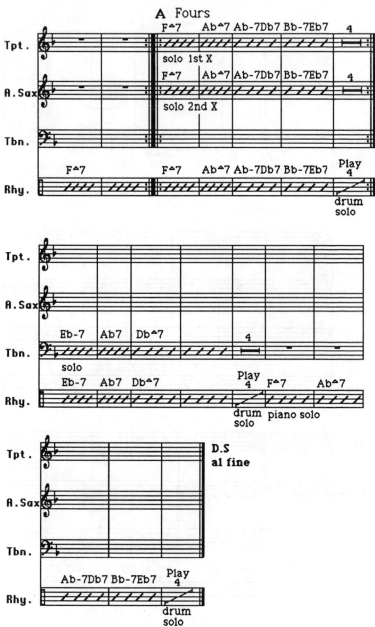

GLOSSARY

Synonyms are given in parentheses after listings.

A SECTION. The first phrase in a tune's chorus structure, most often eight bars long. Subsequent contrasting phrases (using different harmonies and melodies) are labeled "B section," "C section," etc.

ACCENT. Emphasis given to a note, usually by a stronger attack.

ALTERATIONS. Chromatic changes to the diatonic extensions of a chord. For example, F# is the #11 of C7.

ARTICULATION. The manner of interpreting written music. The main considerations are whether a note will be held for its full notated value or less, and whether the note will be accented.

B SECTION (BRIDGE). A contrasting phrase, usually in a thirty-two-bar AABA chorus.

BACKGROUND. A secondary melody (or interval, or chord), simultaneous with the main melody. It is usually made up of long, sustained notes, and is less active than the main melody.

BALLAD. A tune with a slow or very slow tempo, often quiet and subdued in tone and manner.

BLUES. A style of music using a typical chord progression based on the I, IV, and V chords.

BREAK. A short rest, usually one, two, or four bars long, simultaneously played by all members of the group. It is often filled with an improvised solo.

CHANGES (CHORD CHANGES). A chord progression.

CHORUS. A formal unit defined by one complete statement of a tune's chord progression, with or without the melody. A jazz performance will consist of many repetitions of complete statements of the chorus.

COMPING (ACCOMPANYING). Playing the changes on a chordal instrument (piano, guitar, vibes, etc.), complementing and usually secondary to the improvised solo. The specific voicings and rhythms are improvised.

COUNTERPOINT. Two or more simultaneous and equal melodies.

CUE. A discreet signal given by one member of the group during a performance that informs the other members that a prearranged aspect of the arrangement, such as ending a vamp, starting a new tempo or feel, etc., is about to take place. Often used when the exact moment for the change is not predetermined.

CYCLE. A chord progression with a repeated pattern of chords with the same interval between each repetition of the pattern. For example, the progression E-7 A7 D-7 G7 C-7 F7 has a two-chord pattern (II-7 V7) repeated three times with the interval of a whole step between each repetition of the pattern. Commonly used to refer to the following sequence of secondary dominant chords: A7 D7 G7 C7, etc.

DOUBLE-TIME. A change in tempo in which the basic unit of the pulse (usually a quarter note) goes by twice as fast as before.

DOUBLE-TIME FEEL. A change in feel (and, strictly, not a change in tempo) that gives the illusion of double-time, but in which the basic unit of the pulse continues at the same rate.

DOWNBEAT. The first beat in a bar.

EIGHT-BAR PHRASE. A common formal unit in many jazz tunes; for example, an A or B section in a thirty-two-bar AABA tune is an eight-bar phrase.

ENDING. A section of a tune, distinct from and occurring directly after the last statement of the head. Its function is to end the tune.

EXTENSION. The 9th, 11th, or 13th of a chord.

FAKE BOOK. A collection of head charts.

FEEL. The manner of rhythmic interpretation for a tune (i.e., double-time feel). Also used as a synonym for style.

FILL. A very short (one- to four-bar) improvised solo, the function of which is to "fill up" a momentary lull or empty space in the texture.

FORM. Form is determined by the length and number of phrases and the pattern of their repetition. Forms are generally equal to one chorus in length. The two most common forms in jazz are (1) the twelve-bar blues, which has a characteristic chord progression; (2) the thirty-two-bar AABA, which is divided into four eight-bar phrases.

FOURS (TRADING FOURS). The situation in which each successive four-bar segment of a tune is soloed over by a different member of the group, either by rotation among all members of the group, or by alternating with the drummer.

FREE TIME. The suspension or relaxation of a regular pulse.

GUIDE-TONE. The 3rd or 7th of a chord, used to maximize smooth voice-leading between chords.

HALF-TIME. A change in tempo in which the pulse goes by twice as slowly as before.

HALF-TIME FEEL. A change in feel (and, strictly, not a change in tempo) which gives the illusion of half-time, but in which the basic unit of the pulse continues at the same rate.

HARMONIZATION. The process of adding chords (or melodies derived from those chords) to a given melody, usually with the same rhythm as the original melody.

HEAD. One complete statement of the chorus that includes the entire melody.

HEAD ARRANGEMENT. The verbal arranging of a tune by all members of the group. The only written reference, if any, is the head chart.

HEAD CHART (CHART). A musical score that contains only the melody and its accompanying chords notated by chord symbols.

HORN. In jazz, this word has two uses--(1) specifically, a trumpet; (2) in general, any wind instrument.

IMPROVISATION. Spontaneously composing a melody, usually based on practiced patterns, scales, licks, arpeggios, etc.

INTRO. A section of a tune, distinct from and occurring directly before the first statement of the head. Its function is to introduce the tune.

LATIN. A style of jazz, characterized by straight eighth notes and special bass lines and drum patterns (see pages 130-131). Within the Latin style there are further subdivisions, such as samba, bossa nova, etc.

MELODY. In jazz, the previously composed melody played during the head, as opposed to the improvised melody played during a solo.

MUTE. One of several devices inserted into a brass instrument that changes the instrument's tone-color to varying degrees.

OFFBEAT. A rhythm that does not fall on a main beat.

PHRASE. (1) Equal to a formal section, as an A section is often an eight-bar phrase; (2) any melodic unit, often notated by phrase marks that define when wind instruments must breathe.

PICK-UP NOTES. Notes in the melody that occur immediately before the first main downbeat.

PLAY TIME (KEEP TIME) (TIME). A direction given to the drummer to play a standard pattern.

POLYCHORD. A chord consisting of two or more triads or a triad over a bass note (less commonly, two or more seventh chords or triads).

PULSE (BEAT). A series of evenly spaced notes that provide a rhythmic framework. The length of time between any two successive pulses is exactly the same. In jazz, the pulse is usually notated as a quarter note.

RIFF. A short, simple melodic figure that is repeated several times.

RIFF TUNE. A tune whose melody is a riff.

RITARD (RITARDANDO). A gradual slowing of the tempo.

RHYTHM CHANGES. The chord progression to "I Got Rhythm."

RHYTHM SECTION. Those members of the group whose function is to produce a multi-layered harmonic/melodic/rhythmic foundation. This normally includes piano and/or guitar, bass, and drums.

ROCK. A style of jazz, characterized by straight eighth notes and special bass lines and drum patterns (see page 131).

SOLO. An improvised melody.

SOLO BREAK. A break in which a soloist solos. It usually occurs during the last few bars of the previous soloist's last chorus and before the next soloist's first full chorus.

SOLO FILL. A fill in which only one member of the group solos.

STANDARD PATTERN. A basic beat or style that a drummer or a bassist uses as a basis for variation.

STRAIGHT-AHEAD. The style of modern, mainstream jazz that uses standard swing patterns and swing eighth notes.

STRAIGHT EIGHTH-NOTES. A style of interpreting eighth notes in which all eighth notes are interpreted as being the same length, as opposed to swing eighth notes (see Ex. 159).

STYLE. A manner of interpreting jazz. The broadest distinction in style is that between straight eighth note styles, such as Latin and rock, and swing eighth note styles, such as swing or straight-ahead.

SWING EIGHTH NOTES. A style of interpreting eighth notes in which all eighth notes are not interpreted as being the same length, although they are commonly written that way. Swing eighth notes are interpreted as in Ex. 159.

Ex. 159
Swing Eighth Notes

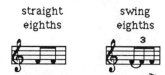

TAG. A turnaround used as an ending.

TEMPO. The rate of the pulse. Tempo is measured by counting the number of pulses occurring within one minute. If a quarter note is the pulse, then the tempo "quarter note = 120" means that one-hundred and twenty quarter notes will occur in one minute. A tempo twice as fast would be two-hundred and forty quarter notes per minute, indicated by "quarter note = 240."

TURNAROUND. A chord progression whose function is to lead back (to "turn around") to the tonic or the beginning of the chorus.

VAMP. A short chord progression repeated indefinitely.

WALKING BASS. In swing style, a bass line using quarter notes and outlining the harmonies with mostly scales and arpeggios.

BIBLIOGRAPHY

ARRANGING

Most of the arranging books listed below emphasize big band or studio arranging (including 4-part voicing), although many topics covered in these books are useful for the small group arranger.

Alexander, Van. *First Chart*. New York: Criterion, 1971.

Baker, David. *Arranging and Composing for the Small Ensemble: Jazz/R&B/Jazz-Rock*. Bloomington, Ind.: Frangipani Press, 1985.

Cacavas, John. *Music Arranging and Orchestration*. Melville, N.Y.: Belwin-Mills Publishing Corp., 1975.

Charlton, Andrew, and De Vries, John M. *Jazz and Commerical Arranging*. 2 vols. Englewood Cliffs, N.J.: Prentice-Hall, 1982.

Collier, Graham. *Compositional Devices, Based on "Songs for My Father."* Boston: Berklee, 1974.

Delamont, Gordon. *Modern Arranging Technique*. Delevan, N.Y.: Kendor Music, 1965.

Deutsch, Maury. *Dr. Deutsch Encyclopedia of Arranging*. New York: Charles Colin, 1977.

Dobbins, Bill. *Jazz Arranging and Composing: A Linear Approach*. Rottenburg, West Germany: Advance Music, 1986.

Garcia, Russell. *The Professional Arranger/Composer*. New York: Criterion Music Corp., 1979.

Grove, Dick. *Arranging Concepts: A Guide to Writing Arrangements for Stage Band Ensembles*. Studio City, Calif.: Dick Grove Publications, 1972.

Houghton, Steve. *A Guide for the Modern Jazz Rhythm Section*. Oskaloosa, Iowa: C. L. Barnhouse, 1982.

Kawakami, Gen'ichi. *Arranging Popular Music: A Practical Guide*. Tokyo: Yamaha Music Foundation, 1975.

Liebman, David. *Lookout Farm: A Case Study of Improvisation for Small Jazz Group* . Hollywood, Calif.: Alamo Publications, 1978.

Mancini, Henry. *Sounds and Scores* . New York: Wise Publications, 1980.

Russo, William. *Composing for the Jazz Orchestra*. Chicago: University of Chicago Press, 1961.

Russo, William. *Jazz Composition and Orchestration*. Chicago: University of Chicago Press, 1968.

Sebesky, Don. *The Contemporary Arranger*. New York: Alfred Publishing Co., 1979.

Taylor, Billy. *Jazz Combo Arranging*. New York: Charles Hansen, 1954.

Wright, Rayburn. *Inside the Score*. Delevan, N.Y.: Kendor Music, 1982.

JAZZ THEORY

Haerle, Dan. *The Jazz Language*. Hialeah, Fla.: Studio 224, 1980.

Haerle, Dan. *Scales for Jazz Improvisation*. Lebanon, Ind.: Studio P/R, 1975.

Ricker, Ramon. *Pentatonic Scales for Jazz Improvisation*. Lebanon, Ind.: Studio P/R, 1975.

Russell, George. *The Lydian Chromatic Concept of Tonal Organization for Improvisation*. New York: Concept Publishing Co., 1959.

Stanton, Kenneth. *Jazz Theory: A Creative Approach*. New York: Taplinger Publishing Co., 1982.

Taylor, Billy. "Jazz Improvisation: 'Rhythm Changes," *Contemporary Keyboard*, October 1977, p. 59.

FAKE BOOKS

Sher, Chuck. *The World's Greatest Fake Book.* San Francisco: Sher Music Co., 1983.

Sher, Chuck. *The New Real Book.* Petaluma, Calif.: Sher Music Co., 1988.

OTHER

Aebersold, Jamey. *Transcribed Piano Voicings: Comping to the Record "A New Approach to Jazz Improvisation, vol. 1."* New Albany, Ind.: Jamey Aebersold, 1980.

Baker, David. *Jazz Improvisation: A Comprehensive Method of Study for All Players.* rev. ed. Bloomington, Ind.: Frangipani Press, 1983.

Brown, Thomas A. *Afro-Latin Rhythm Dictionary.* Sherman Oaks, Calif.: Alfred Publishing Co., Inc., 1984.

Haerle, Dan. *Jazz/Rock Voicings for the Contemporary Keyboard Player.* Lebanon, Ind.: Studio P/R, Inc., 1974.

Read, Gardner. *Music Notation.* Boston: Crescendo, 1969.

DISCOGRAPHY

Listings follow the format below:

Artist. *LP Title*. Label number, date recorded. ℗ and/or ©.
   Tune Title(s) (when cited)

Alternate LP titles and/or label numbers are listed when available.

Abercrombie, John. *Arcade*. ECM-1-1133, 1978. © ℗ 1979 ECM Records GmbH.
   Arcade
Adams, Pepper. *Urban Dreams*. Palo Alto PA 8009, 1981.
   Pent-Up House
Adderly, Cannonball. *Somethin' Else*. Blue Note BST 81595, ca. 1958. © Liberty
   Records, Inc.
   Autumn Leaves
Art Ensemble of Chicago. *Bap-tizum*. Atlantic SD 1639, 1972.
   Odwalla
Art Ensemble of Chicago. *Urban Bushman*. ECM-2-1211, 1980.
   Odwalla
Beirach, Richie. *Eon*. ECM 1054, 1974.
   Nardis
Bellson, Louie. *Raincheck*. Concord CJ-73, ca. 1978.
   Alone Together
Blakey, Art. *Art Blakey and the Jazz Messengers*. Impulse A-7, 1961.
   Invitation
Blakey, Art. *Art Blakey with the Original Jazz Messengers*. Odyssey 32-16-0246, 1956.
   Nica's Dream
Blanchard, Terrence and Donald Harrison. *Discernment*. Concord/George Wein
   Collection GW-3008, 1984.
   When the Saints Go Marchin' In
Bley, Carla. *Live!*. ECM W 12, 1981.
   Song Sung Long

Bley, Carla. *Dinner Music*. Watt/6, 1976.
   Song Sung Long
Blythe, Arthur. *Light Blue: Arthur Blythe Plays Thelonious Monk*. Columbia FC 38661,
   ca. 1983.
   Epistrophy
Blythe, Arthur. *In the Tradition*. Columbia JC 36300, ca. 1979. © 1979 CBS INC./℗
   1979 CBS Inc.
   Naima
Braxton, Anthony. *Trio and Duet*. Sackville 3007, ca. 1973.
   Embraceable You
Brecker Brothers, The. *Some Skunk Funk*. Arista AL 4037, 1975. ℗ & © 1975 Arista
   Records, Inc..
   Some Skunk Funk
Brown, Clifford. *Daahoud*. Mainstream MRL 386, 1954. ℗ 1972 Mainstrem Records.
   Joyspring; Daahoud
Brown, Clifford. *The Immortal Clifford Brown*. Limelight LS 2-8601, 1954.
   Jordu; Joyspring
Brown, Clifford. *The Complete Blue Note and Pacific Jazz Recordings of Clifford
   Brown*. Mosaic MR5-104, 1953.
   Confirmation; Daahoud
Burrell, Kenny. *Moon and Sand*. Concord CJ 121, 1979.
   Stolen Moments
Carter, Betty. *The Audience with Betty Carter*. Bet-Car MK 1003, 1979.
   My Favorite Things
Cole, Richie. *Cool C*. Muse MR 5245, ca. 1981. © ℗ Muse Records.
   Blue Bossa
Cole, Richie and Phil Woods. *Side by Side*. Muse MR 5237, 1980.
   Donna Lee
Coltrane, John. *Afro-Blue Impressions*. Pablo 2620-101, ca. 1962. ℗ 1977 Pablo
   Records.
   Afro-Blue
Coltrane, John. *Blue Train*. Blue Note BST 81577, 1957. © Liberty Records, Inc.
   Blue Train; Moment's Notice
Coltrane, John. *Giant Steps*. Atlantic SD 1311, 1959.
   Giant Steps; Naima
Coltrane, John. *Live at Birdland*. Impulse A-50, 1963.
   Afro-Blue
Coltrane, John. *Live at the Village Vanguard Again!*. Impulse AS-9124, 1966.
   My Favorite Things
Coltrane, John. *My Favorite Things*. Atlantic SD 1361, 1960.
   My Favorite Things
Corea, Chick (Return to Forever). *Light as a Feather*. Polydor PD 5525, ca. 1972.
   500 Miles High; Spain
Corea, Chick. *The Song of Singing*. Blue Note BST 84353, 1970.
   Nefertiti
Corea, Chick. *Trio Music*. ECM 2-1232, 1981.
   'Round Midnight
Davis, Miles. *Cookin' with the Miles Davis Quintet*. Prestige 7094, 1956.
   Airegin (also on *Miles Davis*, Prestige PRT 24001-2 and *Miles Davis Plays Jazz
   Classics*, Prestige 7373)
Davis, Miles. *Greatest Hits*. Prestige PRLP185 & LP 747, 1954.
   Solar (also on *Tune Up*, Prestige P 24077)

Davis, Miles. *Kind of Blue*. Columbia PC 8163, 1959.
   So What
Davis, Miles. *Miles Smiles*. Columbia PC 9401, 1966.
   Footprints; Freedom Jazz Dance
Davis, Miles. *Nefertiti*. Columbia PC 9594, 1967.
   Nefertiti
Davis, Miles. *Relaxin' with the Miles Davis Quintet*. Prestige 7129, 1956.
   Oleo (also on *Miles Davis*, Prestige PRT 24001-2)
Davis, Miles. *Seven Steps to Heaven*. Columbia CS 8851, ca. 1963. © Columbia Records 1963.
   Seven Steps to Heaven
Davis, Miles. *Some Day My Prince Will Come*. Columbia CS 8456, ca. 1961.
   Some Day My Prince Will Come
Davis, Miles. *Sorcerer*. Columbia PC 9532, 1967.
   Sorcerer
Davis, Miles. *Tallest Trees*. Prestige PR 24012, 1954. ℗ 1972 Prestige Records.
   Bag's Groove; Oleo; 'Round Midnight (1956)
Davis, Miles. *Workin' and Steamin'*. Prestige P 24034, 1956. ℗ 1974 Prestige Records.
   Four; Surrey with the Fringe on Top; Well You Needn't
DeJohnette, Jack. *New Directions*. ECM-1-1128, 1978.
   Silver Hollow
Dolphy, Eric. *Outward Bound*. Prestige 7311, ca. 1963.
   On Green Dolphin Street
Duke, George. *A Brazilian Love Affair*. Epic FE 36483, ca. 1979.
   A Brazilian Love Affair
Evans, Bill. *I Will Say Goodbye*. Fantasy F-9593, 1977.
   Dolphin Dance
Evans, Bill. *Spring Leaves*. Milestone M-47034, 1959. © Milestone Records, 1976 ℗ 1976, Milestone Records.
   Autumn Leaves; Spring Is Here; Some Day My Prince Will Come (all also on *Portrait in Jazz*, Riverside 315); *Nardis* (1961, also on *Explorations*, Riverside 351)
Evans, Bill. *The Tokyo Concert*. Fantasy F-9457, 1973.
   On Green Dolphin Street
Evans, Bill. *Peace Piece and Other Pieces*. Milestone 47024, 1959.
   On Green Dolphin Street
Farmer, Art. *The Time And The Place*. Columbia C2 38234, 1967. © 1982 CBS Inc./℗ 1982 CBS Inc.
   Blue Bossa
Farmer, Art and Benny Golson. *Meet the Jazztet*. Chess CH 9159 & Argo LP 664, 1960.
   Killer Joe
Forman, Bruce. *Full Circle*. Concord CJ 251, 1984. ℗ 1984 Concord Jazz, Inc.
   Giant Steps; Summertime
Gillespie, Dizzy. *The Bop Session*. Sonet SNTF 692, 1975. © Sonet Productions Ltd., 1975.
   Confirmation
Gillespie, Dizzy. *The Greatest of Dizzy Gillespie*. RCA Victor LPM 2398, 1946. © by Radio Corporation of America, 1961.
   A Night in Tunisia
Gordon, Dexter. *Manhattan Symphonie*. Columbia JC 35608, ca. 1978. © 1978 CBS Inc./℗ 1978 CBS Inc.
   Body and Soul; Moment's Notice

The Greatest Jazz Concert Ever (Jazz at Massey Hall). Prestige PRST 24024, 1953. ℗
  Prestige Records 1973 .
  Hot House; Salt Peanuts
Grolnick, Don. *Hearts and Numbers*. Hip Pocket HP 106, ca. 1985.
  Pools
Hall, Jim. *Live*. Horizon SP-705, 1975.
  Scrapple from the Apple
Hancock, Herbie. *Headhunters*. Columbia KC 32731, ca. 1973.
  Chameleon; Watermelon Man
Hancock, Herbie. *Maiden Voyage*. Blue Note BST 84195, 1965.
  Eye of the Hurricane; Maiden Voyage
Hancock, Herbie. *VSOP*. Columbia 34688, 1976. © 1977 CBS Inc./℗ 1977 CBS Inc.
  Maiden Voyage
Harris, Eddie. *The Best of Eddie Harris*. Atlantic 1545, 1965. © 1970 Atlantic
  Recording Corporation.
  Freedom Jazz Dance (also on *The In Sound*, Atlantic SD 1448)
Henderson, Joe. *Inner Urge*. Blue Note BST 84189, 1964.
  Inner Urge; Night and Day
Hubbard, Freddie. *Straight Life*. CTI 6007, 1970.
  Here's That Rainy Day; Up Jumped Spring
Hubbard, Freddie. *Red Clay*. CTI 6001 A, 1970.
  Red Clay
Hutcherson, Bobby. *Un Poco Loco*. Columbia FC 36402, ca. 1980.
  Silver Hollow; Un Poco Loco
Hutcherson, Bobby. *In the Vanguard*. Landmark LLP 1513, 1986. ℗ 1987, Landmark
  Records.
  Some Day My Prince Will Come; Well You Needn't
Hutcherson, Bobby. *Good Bait*. Landmark LLP 501, 1984 ℗ 1985 Landmark Records.
  Israel
Jarrett, Keith. *Standards, Vol. 1*. ECM 1255, 1983.
  God Bless the Child
Jobim, Antonio Carlos. *Wave*. A&M SP 3002, 1967.
  Wave
Johnson, J. J. and Kai Winding. *The Great Kai and J. J.* Impulse AS-1, ca. 1955.
  Blue Monk
Jones, Elvin. *Mr. Jones*. Blue Note BN-LA 110-F, 1972.
  New Breed
Kirk, Rahsaan Roland. *Other Folks' Music*. Atlantic SD 1686, ca. 1976.
  Donna Lee
Kuhn, Steve. *Last Year's Waltz*. ECM 1-1213, 1981. © ℗ ECM Records GmbH.
  Confirmation
Lake, Oliver. *The Prophet*. Black Saint BSR 0044, 1980.
  The Prophet
Liebman, Dave (Quest). *Quest*. Palo Alto PA 8061, 1981.
  Lonely Woman
Liebman, Dave. *Pendulum*. 1978, Artists House AH 9408.
  Footprints
Lloyd, Charles. *Forest Flower*. Atlantic SD 1473, 1966. © Atlantic Recording
  Corporation.
  Forest Flower
Lorber, Jeff. *Galaxian*. Arista AL 9545, ca. 1981.
  Magic Lady

Martino, Pat. *Exit.* Muse MR 5075, 1976.
   Blue Bossa
McLaughlin, John (Mahavishnu Orchestra). *Inner Mounting Flame.* Columbia KC 31067, 1971.
   Meeting of the Spirits
McPherson, Charles. *The Quintet Live!.* Prestige 7480, 1966.
   Here's That Rainy Day
McRae, Carmen. *The Great American Songbook.* Atlantic SD 2-904, ca. 1972.
   Satin Doll
McRae, Carmen. *At the Great American Music Hall.* Blue Note BNLA 709-H2, 1976.
   On Green Dolphin Street
Metheny, Pat. *As Falls Wichita, So Falls Wichita Falls.* ECM 1-1190, 1980.
   As Falls Wichita, So Falls Wichita Falls
Metheny, Pat. *Watercolors.* ECM 1-1097, 1977.
   Lakes; Watercolors
Metheny, Pat. *80/81.* ECM 2-1180, 1980.
   80/81, Two Folk Songs: 1st
Metheny, Pat. *Song X.* Geffen GHS 24096, 1985.
   Kathelin Gray
Metheny, Pat. *Pat Metheny Group.* ECM-1-1114, 1978. © ℗ 1978 ECM Records GMBH.
   April Joy
Mingus, Charles. *Jazz Workshop.* Savoy 12059; Savoy SJL 1113, 1954. ℗ & © 1977 Arista Records.
   Tea for Two
Mingus, Charles. *Mingus.* Prestige PR 24010, no date.
   All the Things You Can C Sharp; Ladybird
Mingus, Charles. *Better Git It in Your Soul.* Columbia G 30628, no date.
   Mood Indigo
Mitchell, Blue. *A Blue Time.* Milestone M-47055, 1959. ℗ 1980, Milestone Records.
   Nica's Dream
Mobley, Hank. *Messages.* Prestige 7061; P-24063, 1956.
   52nd Street Theme
Mobley, Hank. *Straight No Filter.* Blue Note BST 84435, 1966.
   Chain Reaction
Modern Jazz Quartet, The. *First Recordings.* Prestige 7749, 1952.
   All the Things You Are; Django
Modern Jazz Quartet, The. *The Art of the Modern Jazz Quartet/The Atlantic Years.* Atlantic SD2-301, 1962.
   Lonely Woman (also on *Lonely Woman*, Atlantic LP 1381)
Modern Jazz Quartet, The. *The Modern Jazz Quartet.* Atlantic SD 1265, ca. 1957.
   Bag's Groove; Night in Tunisia
Monk, Thelonious. *At the Five Spot.* Milestone M-47043, 1958. ℗ 1977, Milestone Records.
   In Walked Bud
Monk, Thelonious. *Blues Five Spot.* Milestone M-9124, 1958.
   'Round Midnight
Monk, Thelonious. *The Complete Genius.* Blue Note BNLA 579-H2, 1948. © ℗ MCMLXXVI United Artists Music and Records Group, Inc.
   All the Things You Are; Epistrophy; Misterioso
Monk, Thelonious. *Live at the Jazz Workshop.* Columbia C2 38269-70, 1964. © 1982 CBS Inc./℗ 1982 CBS Inc.
   'Round Midnight

Monk, Thelonious. *Monk*. Original Jazz Classics OJC-016, 1954.
   Smoke Gets in Your Eyes
Montgomery, Wes. *The Small Group Recordings*. Verve VE-2-2513, 1965.
   Impressions
Morgan, Frank. *Easy Living*. Contemporary C-14013, ca. 1985. ℗ 1985, Fantasy, Inc.
   Yes and No
Morgan, Frank. *Bebop Lives!*. Contemporary C-14026, 1986. ℗ 1987, Fantasy, Inc.
   All the Things You Are
Mouzon, Alphonse. *Love, Fantasy*. 1987, MPC 6001.
   Milestones
Murphy, Mark. *Stolen Moments*. Muse MR 5102, 1978. © ℗ 1978 Muse Records.
   Stolen Moments
Murray, David. *New Life*. Black Saint BSR 0100, 1985.
   Blues in the Pocket
Nelson, Oliver. *Blues and the Abstract Truth*. Impulse AS-5, 1961. Pub. by Noslen
   Music Co.--BMI.
   Stolen Moments
Newton, James. *The African Flower*. Blue Note BT 85109, 1985.
   Cotton Tail
Out of the Blue. *Inside Track*. Blue Note BT 85128, 1986.
   Hot House
Parker, Charlie. *Bird/The Savoy Recordings*. Savoy 2201, 1945. ℗ © 1976 Arista
   Records, Inc.
   Now's the Time
Parker, Charlie. *The Verve Years (1952-1954)*. Verve VE-2-2523, 1953. © ℗ 1977
   Polydor Incorporated.
   Confirmation
Parker, Charlie. *The Very Best of Bird*. Warner Bros. 2WB 3198, 1947.
   Cool Blues
Peterson, Oscar. *Live at the Northsea Jazz Festival*. Pablo 2620-15, 1980. ℗ 1981,
   Pablo Records, Inc..
   Caravan; Straight No Chaser
Powell, Bud. *The Amazing Bud Powell*. Blue Note BST 81503, 1951.
   Un Poco Loco
Puente, Tito. *Mambo Diablo*. Concord Picante CJP-283, 1985. ℗ 1985 Concord
   Picante.
   Take Five
Puente, Tito. *El Rey*. Concord Picante CJP-250, 1984.
   Autumn Leaves; Equinox
Puente, Tito. *Sensación*. Concord Picante CJP-301, ca. 1986.
   Jordu; 'Round Midnight
Redman, Dewey. *Soundsigns*. Galaxy GXY-5130, 1978. ℗ 1981 Galaxy Records.
   Half Nelson
Roach, Max. *Chattahoochee Red*. Columbia FC 37376, ca. 1981. © 1981 CBS Inc./℗
   1981 CBS Inc.
   Giant Steps
Rollins, Sonny. *Sonny Rollins on Impulse!*. Impulse AS-91, 1965.
   On Green Dolphin Street
Rollins, Sonny. *Saxophone Colossus and More*. Prestige P 24050, 1956. © 1975, Pres-
   tige Records.
   Blue Seven; St. Thomas (both also on *Saxophone Colossus*, Prestige 7326); *Pent-
   Up House* (also on *Sonny Rollins Plus Four*, Prestige 7038)

Russell, George. *Outer Thoughts*. Milestone M-47027, 1962.
  Au Privave; You Are My Sunshine (also on *The Outer View*, Riverside 440);
    'Round Midnight (also on *Ezz-thetics*, Riverside 375)
Sample, Joe. *The Three*. Inner City IC 6007, 1975. ℗ 1978 Inner City Records.
  On Green Dolphin Street; Satin Doll
Sanchez, Poncho. *Papa Gato*. Concord CJP-310, 1986.
  Jumpin' with Symphony Sid
Santamaria, Mongo. *Red Hot*. Columbia 35696, 1979.
  Watermelon Man
Scofield, John. *Live*. Inner City 3022, 1977.
  Leaving
Scofield, John. *Who's Who*. Arista AN 3018, ca. 1979.
  Cassidae
Shorter, Wayne. *Adam's Apple*. Blue Note BST 84232, 1967.
  Footprints
Sidran, Ben. *Bop City*. Antilles AN 1012A, 1983. ℗ 1983 Island Records Inc.
  Solar
Silver, Horace. *Song for My Father*. Blue Note BLP 84185, ca. 1964.
  The Kicker; Song for My Father
Stadler, Heiner. *A Tribute to Monk and Bird*. Tomato TOM-2-9002-A, 1978.
  *Air Conditioning; Au Privave; Ba-lue Bolivar Ba-lues-are; Misterioso; Straight
    No Chaser*
Steps Ahead. *Steps Ahead*. Elektra/Musician 60168-A, 1983.
  Pools
Stitt, Sonny. *Genesis*. Prestige P-24044, P-7077, ca. 1950.
  Cherokee
Tjader, Cal. *La Onda Va Bien*. Concord CJP-113, 1979. ℗ 1980 Concord Jazz, Inc.
  Serengeti
Turrentine, Stanley. *The Baddest Turrentine*. CTI 6005, 1970, 1971. ℗ 1972, 1973,
    Creed Taylor, Inc.
  Sugar (1970, also on *Sugar* CTI 6005); *Salt Song* (1971, also on *Salt Song* CIT
    6010)
Tyner, McCoy. *Nights of Ballads and Blues*. Impulse AS-39, 1963.
  Blue Monk
Tyner, McCoy. *Reaching Forth*. Impulse AS-33, 1962.
  Have You Met Miss Jones
Tyner, McCoy. *Song for My Lady*. Milestone MSP 9044, 1972.
  The Night Has a Thousand Eyes
Tyner, McCoy. *Supertrios*. Milstone M-55003, 1977.
  Stella by Starlight; Wave
Tyner, McCoy. *Today and Tomorrow*. Impulse AS-63, 1963.
  Autumn Leaves
Walton, Cedar. *Eastern Rebellion*. Timeless Muse TI 306, 1975.
  Naima
Washington, Grover. *A Secret Place*. Kudu KU-32 S1, 1976.
  Dolphin Dance
Weather Report. *Black Market*. Columbia 34099, no date.
  Barbary Coast; Gibraltar; Elegant People; Three Clowns
Weather Report. *Heavy Weather*. Columbia 34418, ca. 1977.
  Palladium
Weather Report. *I Sing the Body Electric*. Columbia 31352, 1972.
  Second Sunday in August

Weather Report. *Mr. Gone.* Columbia PC 35358, ca. 1978.
   Mr. Gone
Weather Report. *Mysterious Traveller.* Columbia 32494, ca. 1974.
   American Tango; Mysterious Traveller; Nubian Sundance; Scarlet Woman
Weather Report. *Sweetnighter.* Columbia 32210, ca. 1973.
   Boogie Woogie Waltz; Manolete; Non-Stop Home; 125th Street Congress; Will;
Winter, Paul (The Winter Consort). *Road.* A&M SP 4279, ca. 1972. ℗ 1972 CBS, Inc.
   Icarus
Woods, Phil. *Altology.* Prestige P-24065, 1957.
   Solar (also on *Bird Feathers,* New Jazz 8204)
Woods, Phil. *Birds of a Feather.* Antilles AN 1006-B, 1981. ℗ 1982 Island Records,
   Inc.
   Nica's Dream
Woods, Phil. *Bird's Night.* Savoy SJL 2257 or Savoy MG 12138, 1957.
   Scrapple from the Apple
Woods, Phil. *The Phil Woods Quartet Volume 1.* Clean Cuts CL 702, 1979. ℗ & ©
   1980 Clean Cuts, Inc.
   Along Came Betty; Hallucinations
Yellowjackets, The. *Mirage à Trois.* Warner Bros. 1-23813, no date.
   I Got Rhythm

INDEX OF TUNES

Entries are listed in the following format:

Tune Title
    Arranging technique; Artist; *LP Title(s)*   page #

Artist and LP title are only given for those tunes that
refer to a specific recording.

GENERAL INDEX